AF617896

Tender

Digitality

" [...]

(ed.)
CHARLOTTE
AXELSSON

slanted

Table of Content

Tender Digitality, Charlotte Axelsson 4
Castle, Sascha Schneider 14
Playification. The Recall on Gamification, Mela Kocher 16
Backup and Beyond, Hannah Eßler 24
Can You Hear It Splashing? Marcial Koch 32
Dance Score Weave, Friederike Lampert 40
Tactile Media, Oliver Ruf 48
Take Care — Thoughts on Tenderness in the Digital Age, Marie-France Rafael 56
The Loneliness of the Female Astronaut, Oliver Bendel 60
Transitions and Thresholds, Francis Müller 62
The Night Remains, Leoni Hof 68
Empty and Space, Marisa Burn 72
The New Research Program, Alexander Damianisch 78
Traces of a Lost Relationship, Léa Ermuth 84
Relate to Someone, Barbara Getto 90
Synthetic Tenderness, Grit Wolany 96
Mirror, Mirror on the Wall, Gunter Lösel 104
Reflecting on Oneself, Dana Blume 114

ENDPAPERS: Underwater, Oliver Brunko
INTRO TEXTS: Charlotte Axelsson

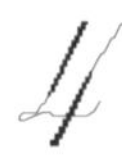

Charlotte Axelsson

Tender Digitality

‹Our intuition works very well in the analogue sphere, and we now also need to hone it in the digital one.›[1]

Charlotte Axelsson explores ‹tender digitality› as an aesthetically-centred concept – one she initially engaged with as part of a 2019 workshop titled ‹Smart Setting›. She has been thinking about ways to articulate and cultivate sensuality, perception, intuition, and well-being in digital contexts ever since.

Charlotte Axelsson is Head of E-Learning, Learning & Teaching Dossier at the Zurich University of the Arts and is writing her dissertation at the University of Zurich.

Tender Digitality

Closing your eyes while reading is not usually helpful, but I'd like to invite you to close your eyes for a moment before you start reading this text. I'll be referencing "Listening to Data Flows"[2] here, a research project that explores the sound data makes. Perhaps it's something like a gentle whoosh, hooeee. A subtle bonk, shooosh. Can you hear it, dear reader? Are you a listening reader now?

It is common practice in the field of design to question and clarify terms and concepts before moving on to their practical application. This may have its origins in philosophers such as Michel Foucault, whose work is often referred to in design, art, and cultural studies as a fundamental framework for the creative process. According to Foucault's theory, statements are always considered in context, and the dynamics between them evolve uniquely for each individual as the context changes. A name or term, in this view, serves as a kind of container, offering new meanings depending on how it is used. Foucault goes on to explain that this distinctive connection has the ability to transform a statement, even if it's the same sentence, depending solely on when the reader encounters it, even when the same rules of interpretation are applied.[3]

Providing initial explanations for terms establishes at the very least a basis for comprehension and understanding. Recognising that texts are uniquely interpreted each time, defining these terms provides an excellent opportunity to minimise misunderstandings and steer the perceptual scope in a direction favoured by the creator. Clarifying terms is thus a first aesthetic gesture in the creative process, a tender feeling-one's-way into an abstract world. Vilém Flusser's concept of "things and non-things" dovetails with this notion. The philosopher, with his phenomenological conceptual analyses, paints vivid pictures in our minds and encourages us to discover unexpected elements within the ordinary and familiar. He illuminates environments and details what happens when objects are taken out of their original context and cultural milieu. Things are transformed into "non-things" – a shift that serves to de-vulgarise the vulgar.[4]

The following essay subscribes to these lines of thought and seeks to construct an aesthetic space of understanding. It associates digitalisation, the digital and digitality with tenderness. These four terms are taken out of their usual context, observed and perhaps even their conventions altered. The text culminates in an amalgamation, intertwined with observations and a touch of playfulness. The depiction of these four terms bears a resemblance to the research project "Listening to Data Flows"[5], generating as it does a sensory-aesthetic hum that paints pictures within awakened synapses.

Digital refers to an electronic signalling
process used to generate something.

A brief linguistic detour from this tentative analysis reveals the etymological origins of the word "digital" in the Latin term *digitalis*[6], meaning "pertaining to the fingers": [M]id-15c., "pertaining to numbers below ten;" 1650s, "pertaining to fingers," from Latin *digitalis,* from *digitus* "finger or toe" [...]. The numerical sense is because numerals under 10 were counted on fingers. Meaning "using numerical digits" is from 1938, especially of computers which run on data in the form of digits (opposed to *analogue)* after c. 1945. In reference to recording or broadcasting, from 1960.[7] The derivation is also evident at the metaphorical level. As a linguistic bridge from the tender to the digital, it evokes both a specific, concrete image – creating code with one's finger, sliding and moving a finger across a touchscreen, feeling the vibrations of a smartphone in your trouser pocket – and an abstract one: touching virtual worlds, forging synthetic relationships, shaping artificial intelligences, navigating digital realms. Bearing this aesthetic understanding in mind, we move on to the next concept.

Digitalisation is a technological and
electronic process of transformation.

Throughout history, there have been pivotal moments that ushered in profound developments or, as Dirk Baecker puts it, organisational "catastrophes" to which society must find an answer.[8] Turning points such as the Lascaux cave paintings, for example, the invention of the camera obscura, the films of the Lumière brothers or the first photograph by Joseph Niépce, the advent of the iPhone and the emergence of pre-trained Transformer models such as ChatGPT all are innovations having to do with reproducing, expanding, and reimagining communication. They are also a harbinger not only of technological change and advancement, but also of social and cultural change. Each of these transformations alters the existing state of affairs and forges a new, more abstract reality. These are not isolated developments, of course, but complex conglomerates of various movements. Felix Stalder approaches this development from a cultural perspective,[9] arguing that technological advances arise from the needs of societies and cultures. This, in turn, leads to the creation of technological developments that subsequently serve as fertile ground for the cultivation of cultures. According to Stalder, *digitalisation* is the process of transforming tangible entities into an electrified, coded state, achieved through the influence of impulses that ultimately manifest as binary signals in the digital realm.

> *Digitality* is the interplay between technology and humanity, encompassing social and cultural change.

Digitality refers to the cultural process of change, a transformation initiated by society. We change (ourselves and other things), and we are changed. We currently find ourselves in a technological liminal space, immersed in abstract worlds, navigating a multiplicity of realities within generational divides. We encounter a new understanding of time and space at a new pace. We understand tenderness as a deeply serious and aesthetic moment.[10] This brings us to the next conceptual container, namely *tenderness* – the tender as an aesthetic moment that shows us the contours of the in-between, of that which is hardly tangible. It encompasses a wide range of interpretations and attempts to encapsulate a feeling that, in truth, defies description. It is at once intimate and projected outwards. Roland Barthes characterises this interplay as a sensual engagement with the concept of *pleasure*. He explores the interdependence between the creator and the consumer – one being the individual and the object that provides a space for pleasure, the other being the one who navigates that space through the lens of pleasure.[11] He further shows how this sense of pleasure is intimately linked to physicality, also extending into the realm of the erotic.[12] Or, as Catherine Hakim defines it, erotic capital: “capital” in this context refers to a combination of various attributes, encompassing aesthetic, visual, physical, social and sexual attractiveness.[13] What's intriguing about Hakim's approach is that she categorises these interactions into six or seven competencies, some of which can be acquired, involve cultural structures, or depend on one's initial physical disposition. If we compare these descriptions of the concepts of lust and eroticism with that of tenderness, they all represent aesthetic states of the unconscious, of emotion. Lust and eroticism are intertwined with states of tension that demand, expect, and require certain interactions. Tenderness, on the other hand, reflects a tender perception of physicality, namely one that observes, shapes, and describes togetherness. Şeyda Kurt playfully explores this complexity in her alternative alphabet of tenderness, from "A" for affection to "L" for laziness, "S" for solidarity and "V" for vulnerability.[14] Her reflections on radical tenderness underscore both how multimodal this emotional moment of tenderness is and the profound power it holds.

From this perspective, tenderness can be regarded as the primordial mother of sensuality, combining as it does elements of both eroticism and pleasure by placing bodily awareness at the centre. Tenderness strives for unity and selflessness; it is competition-free. This intrinsic quality is what makes tenderness so potent and seductive, especially when juxtaposed with digitality in a world that exists primarily in a disembodied state. Tender digitality brings a sense of physicality and sensibility to the digital realm. This revelation introduces new concepts to the culture of digitality[15] and potentially provides answers that we need to seek in this transitional phase, as we move from one possibility to another[16] in the transition "from order to disorder and from disorder to order", as Baecker calls it in his study of the coming society.[17] And so, with the concept of tender digitality, we also discuss the role of the human in the digital. Such a discussion opens up space for exploration at a time when the world and humanity are grappling with uncertainty, the palpable effects of the climate crisis, and extreme manifestations of consumerism, not to mention a sense of anxiety about the future that weighs heavily on younger generations. It is a time when the job market is changing rapidly and radically, educational institutions are facing profound challenges, and individuals are seeking answers to key questions about their purpose in the context of artificial intelligence.

Let's take a moment to reflect on the importance of infusing these transitional spaces with a tender digitality: how do we navigate the digital realm – with playfulness, empathy, or through new forms of collaboration? It is an approach that naturally brings initially atypical conceptual constellations into de-vulgarised relations. When we consider tenderness as a culturally evolved moment, it creates a link between humanity and digitalisation. It gives the *human homo digitalis* its sensory, aesthetic and experiential domain, while at the same time creating a digital space within the analogue. Here we might take a cue from Goethe's *Faust,* allowing ourselves to turn the original statement into a question: "Here I am Man – dare man to be"?[18]

This user practice of tender digitality involves the art of finding one's way and navigating a virtual world while existing in a disembodied state – a process characterised by sensing, orienting, and fluid movement. It is important not to confuse this with the phenomenon of immersion, which involves being drawn into alternative realities or a feeling of "flow" that causes you forget your surroundings.[19] Consequently, this observation raises several interrelated questions: What does it mean to navigate digital space? How does it differ from analogue navigation, and where are the parallels? What new skills emerge from this process, and how can they be nurtured and honed?

To answer these questions, it is worth describing navigation in non-digital, analogue space. In analogue space, our bodies move more or less in a linear fashion, straightforwardly traversing demarcated boundaries from point A to point B. We travel through time, move from one place to another, we are born and die. Consequently, the most fascinating bodily processes are the non-linear ones – the organised chaos of order and disorder within our brains that makes our surroundings perceptible in the first place. The brain serves as the body's control centre, an information-processing hub that receives input from multisensory receptors responsible for our perception. It processes stimuli, interprets information, and directs our attention to reality. This rotation is central to constructivist theory, which describes aesthetic sensation as the starting point for experiencing the world. Under the framework of Gestalt psychology, this sensory input is categorised and classified. The assumption is that

“ [...]
don’t forget
to be kind
↘
and show tenderness
to all,
⁂
to behave
as a
tender homo digitalis
would.
⁑

while our body does indeed move in a line from point A to point B in analogue space, our experience of this movement is multi-dimensional due to the input from our sensory perceptions. Perception itself is an aesthetic experience – in other words, aesthetics encapsulates the domain of the senses and behaves, as Hanne Appelqvist argues, contrary to the conceptual realm of logic.[20]

Applying this concept to digital navigation, we can say that in the digital realm we are essentially "bodyless" and heavily reliant on our senses. As a result, the "linear, analogue physicality" of digital space is transformed into an "aesthetic, digitalised physicality". For the culture of digitality, this means a transformation or concentration of the traditional linear description of processes influenced by the physical body. As described earlier with the concepts of digitalisation and digitality, technology continues to evolve, enabling multidimensionality and, at the same time, the parallel or polyrhythmic development of cultural and social structures.

These changes are particularly noticeable in learners. They are here, there, everywhere all at once, seem to lack concentration and are easily distracted. One assumption is that they are moving away from linear thinking patterns. This could be seen as an indication of the perceptual multidimensionality that occurs in digital domains, a trait that they also carry over to the realm of physical objects. The development is further enhanced by technologies such as artificial neural networks (ANNs), which are inspired by biological neurons and allow the computational power of natural brains to be harnessed for digital purposes.[21]

It follows that the architecture of ANNs is not based on "linear" processes, but rather on multimodal networks that are interconnected22 in a multidimensional way. It is this architecture that enables, for example, ChatGPT to generate such surprisingly coherent content, or Midjourney to produce remarkably high-quality images. Another technological advance worth mentioning is that of the qubit, or quantum bit: the signals of qubits are no longer computed in a linear or binary way; the underlying structure is multidimensional and rooted in the principles of quantum physics. While quantum computers are still far from being readily available to the general public, this example illustrates how chaos and multidimensionality are fundamental requirements of digitisation and directly influence how we navigate digital space.

The question is, how do we navigate these contexts, how does the human role evolve, and what are the implications of transhumanism[23] for humanity? How can we educate people in a way that allows them to navigate both worlds? Perhaps it's also about embracing the idea that tender digitality means learning to actively shape and occupy those in-between spaces within both worlds. We are hybrid beings, navigating realms through artificial neural networks, transcending time and space while remaining in constant interaction. In contemplating tender digitality, we delve deeper into the question of what it truly means to be human.[24] This tenderness in the digital domain is important, as we tend to focus so much on technology that we forget to act like a human being. Perhaps that is where a follow-up is in order, specifically in terms of play, empathy, collaboration.

Play

The digital domain is the incubator of play, and play[25] takes digital form: press a key to surf the ethernet, follow unknown paths though links and playfully navigate a binary system – float, surf, fly, transport yourself into multiple worlds; see blinking, listen to interesting sounds, jump and run – act like a person who doesn't exist, hide behind avatars or become a living cyborg yourself, predict the future and archive the past, die fast and live forever, imagine walking on clouds – press keys to be alone or in a swarm of different societies and cultures, to react and create, twinkle twinkle little star, find yourself where the beginnings of protopia[26] may start and dystopia may end. The digital domain is a playground; fasten your seatbelt and prepare yourself for it, but don't forget to be human, don't forget to be kind and show tenderness to all, to behave as a tender *homo digitalis* would.

Empathy

not to mention all the other forgotten words starting with "e": equal, emancipation, exploration, experiment, exhausted, e(i)rregular, electronic, easy, else, erotic. emerge, engage, ever, ethernet, Earth, ego, eggs, establishment, education, endless, exit.

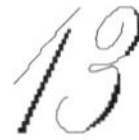

Collaboration
co l lab oration
co lab l oriaton
lab loriaton co
lor ton co at aibl
to lab or laction

1. Charlotte Axelsson in conversation with Ruth Frischknecht, see Leoni Hof, "Structural Change", ZHdK, July 12, 2023, www.zhdk.ch/en/news/structural-change-6597
2. The project, directed by Hannes Rickli, is taking place at the Institute for Contemporary Art Research (IFCAR) at the Zurich University of the Arts (ZHdK) from June 2021 to May 2024. See "Listening to Data Flows: How Art and Biology Bring the Environment into the Computer", ZHdK, accessed July 17, 2023, www.zhdk.ch/en/researchproject/582235
3. See Michel Foucault, *The Archaeology of Knowledge,* trans. A. M. Sheridan Smith (New York: Pantheon, 1972), 25–29.
4. See Vilém Flusser, *The Shape of Things: A Philosophy of Design* (Munich: Carl Hanser, 1993), 85–86.
5. See "Listening to Data Flows".
6. "digital," Merriam Webster, accessed October 15, 2023, www.merriam-webster.com/dictionary/digital
7. "digital (adj.)", Etymonline, accessed July 26, 2023, www.etymonline.com/word/digital
8. Dirk Baecker, *Studien zur nächsten Gesellschaft* (Frankfurt am Main: Suhrkamp, 2018), 34.
9. See Felix Stalder, Kultur der Digitalität (Frankfurt am Main: Suhrkamp, 2006).
10. See Mela Kocher and Charlotte Axelsson, "Digitale Didaktik: Neupositionierung der Hochschuldidaktik", in *Kompetenzentwicklung in kooperativen Netzwerken: LeLa – LernLabor Hochschuldidaktik,* ed. Charlotte Axelsson, Dana Blume, and Benno Volk (Bielefeld: transcript, 2024), 333–52, here 342.
11. See Roland Barthes, *The Pleasure of the Text,* trans. Richard Miller (New York: Hill and Wang, 1975), 17–25.
12. See ibid.
13. See Catherine Hakim, "Erotic Capital", *European Sociological Review* 26, no. 5 (2010): 499–518.
14. Şeyda Kurt, *Radikale Zärtlichkeit: Warum Liebe politisch ist* (Berlin: HarperCollins, 2021).
15. See Felix Stalder, *Kultur der Digitalität* (Frankfurt am Main: Suhrkamp, 2006).
16. See Baecker, *Studien zur nächsten Gesellschaft,* 39.
17. Ibid.
18. Johann Wolfgang von Goethe, *Faust,* trans. Bayard Taylor (Cleveland: World Publishing Company, 2005), 65 (verse 940), Project Gutenberg, www.gutenberg.org/files/14591/14591-h/14591-h.htm
19. Christian Iseli in conversation with Charlotte Axelsson, "What the Digital?! 3 – Gespräch mit Christian Iseli über Immersion", Modcast, ZHdK, March 21, 2022, www.modcast.zhdk.ch/m/wtd3-christian-iseli, ca. 7:00.
20. See Hanne Appelqvist, "Ästhetik", in *Wittgenstein-Handbuch: Leben – Werk – Wirkung,* ed. Anja Weiberg and Stefan Majetschak (Stuttgart: Metzler, 2022), 181–88, here 181.
21. See Marc Engenhart and Sebastian Löwe, *Design und künstliche Intelligenz: Theoretische und praktische Grundlagen der Gestaltung mit maschinell lernenden Systemen* (Basel: Birkhäuser, 2022), 30–31.
22. See ibid., 44–45.
23. BBC, "I'm transhuman. I'm going to become digital – BBC", YouTube video, May 14, 2019, 3:15, youtu.be/qOcktbXSfxU?feature=shared, here 2:27.
24. See The Agency, "Die Gestaltung des Übermenschlichen: Was bedeutet es, human zu sein?", in *Ich, wir & Digitalität: Eine ethische Auseinandersetzung,* ed. Charlotte Axelsson (Kölliken: buch & netz, 2021), 25–29, here 25.
25. See Mela Kocher's article in this volume: 16.
26. See Kevin Kelly, *What Technology Wants.* (New York: Viking Press, 2010)

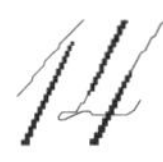

Sascha Schneider

Castle

Sascha Schneider explores how we learn, or rather how and where digital materials can support or disrupt the learning process. He brings expertise to the field of learning with his mindful thinking and experimental approach, which he calls Cognitive-Affective-Social Theory of Learning in digital Environments, or {CASTLE} for short. When we talk about tenderness in digital learning, sensory memory is where the magic happens. Find your way through the concatenation of circumstances in this maze that is the learning process.

Sascha Schneider is Professor for Educational Technology at the Institute of Education at the University of Zurich.

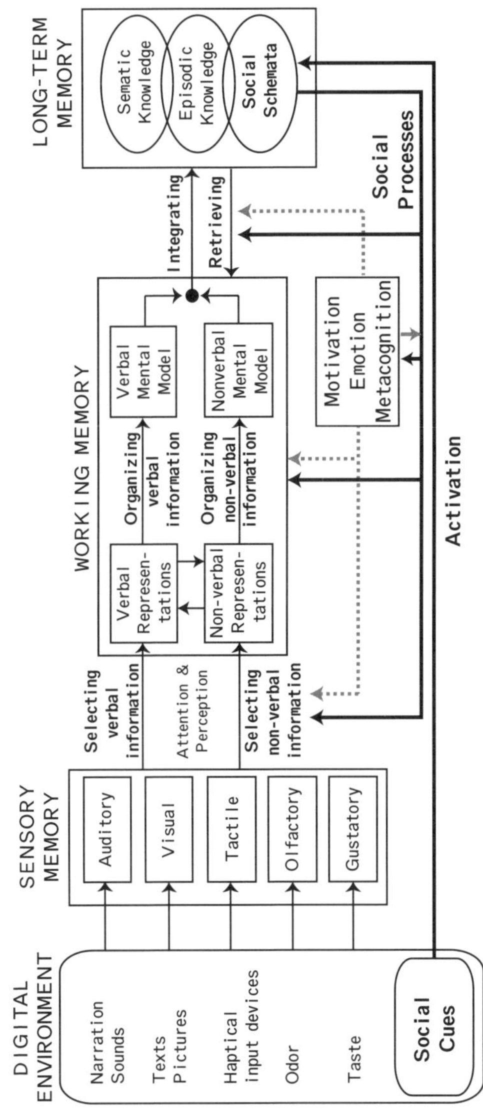

Schneider, S., Beege, M., Nebel, S. et al. (2022). The Cognitive-Affective-Social Theory of Learning in digital Environments (CASTLE). *Educational Psychology Review,* 34, 1–38. doi.org/10.1007/s10648-021-09626-5

Mela Kocher

Playification. The Recall On Gamification

Is there really just one right way to hold a spoon? Could this be a game, are you a player, and what does Friedrich Schiller have to do with Mela Kocher? Choose a path and play your way through what amounts to a text full of possibilities. Think of each conclusion as a pause, not an endpoint. A platform game, a jump 'n' run, with Kocher asking you to run on and on in the name of play. But what can I say: just play, enter the game.

Mela Kocher is project manager for ludic didactics in the E-Learning, Learning & Teaching Dossier of the Zurich University of the Arts and teaches on the Master's programme in Game Design at the ZHdK.

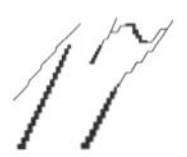

Tutorial

"Man only plays when he is in the fullest sense of the word a human being, and he is only fully a human being when he plays", Friedrich Schiller wrote almost 230 years ago in his letters *On the Aesthetic Education of Man* – a description of the human urge to play that continues to resonate.[1] Looking at the practice of play in children and adults globally, as well as in animals, it is evident that play can be a source of emotional and motivational strength, inspiration, and creativity.[2] Its tentacles, like those of a jellyfish or seaweed,[3] reach far: far beyond scoring points and chasing leaderboards, beyond data collection, learning quizzes, self-optimisation and assessment – and, as you might have guessed, far beyond gamification. "It's like reducing cuisine to nutrition", game designer and scholar Eric Zimmerman scoffed in his short essay "Against Gamification".[4]

Gamification is commonly understood as "the process of adding games or gamelike elements to something (such as a task) so as to encourage participation"[5]. The attempt to harness the power of play so as to magically enhance any kind of activity has, over the years, been reduced to the infamous "points, badges and leaderboard" formula.[6] It is a hollow promise and not as effective as it intends to be – studies have long shown that poorly designed extrinsic motivation devalues the content and can therefore backfire.[7]

But let's not throw the baby out with the bathwater! The following suggests a recall and proposes the concept of "playification" – radically opposing gamification paradigms by exploring the impact of games and play literacies in other ways.

Reading Instructions

This text can be read in several ways:

- **You can play it like "snakes and ladders", jumping forwards and backwards whenever you see an arrow pointing somewhere.**
- **You can answer the personality type questions at the beginning of a "level" and be directed to a particular section in that "level", then move on to the next "level" and so on, reading half of the essay.**
- **Or you can do whatever you like!**

Level 1: Enter the Magic Circle: Jump Down the Rabbit Hole

When defining a phenomenon, it is instructive to look at it from different angles. The concept of "play" is a wobbly one and difficult to define – as demonstrated by Hans-Georg Gadamer's hermeneutics, Ludwig Wittgenstein's philosophy of language, and Katie Salen and Eric Zimmerman's rules of play, each of which ascribes different characteristics to "play".[8] So where do we begin? Our playification oracle will help you find the right starting point. Please answer the following question:

What's on your mind?

- All this talk about playification! What does it really mean? [→ go to Definitions]
  or
- I like playing cards or board games. But where else can I play? [→ go to Examples]

Definitions

Playification can be seen as a mindset, a method, or phenomenon. As a *mindset,* it describes the ludic attitude[9] of subverting processes, uncovering subtleties, creating new meaning – by playing! As a *method,* playification is the application of playful sparks and methods in non-game contexts, such as using randomness or role-playing, swapping places, twisting rules, performing strange experiments [→ go to Methods]. Gamification, as it is mostly understood today,[10] derives its (marketing and assessment) power from the generation

Examples

Play can happen (almost) anywhere, and open-ended applications in particular tend to be playified. An example might be an applied game card set that offers a variety of game play possibilities, such as "Ideas for Games", an idea-generating card set for game designers.[12] Approaches that focus on randomness are also part of the playification culture.[13] For a literary example, read the novel *Dice Man* (1971) for a fascinating look at a manically dice-induced cult. Decision-making can easily be facilitated through play, and so a sense of of data/a quantifiable outcome. It aims to increase motivation by extrinsic means, through the application of the above-mentioned "points – badges – leaderboard". School grades are a good example of this. As a *phenomenon,* the focus of playification is to promote a meaningful experience by creating an intervention.[11] The difference between gamification and playification can be defined as follows: Where gamification aims to change the attitude of participants, playification aims to change the experience itself.

joyful anticipation can easily be injected into an otherwise uneventful sequence of work steps (e.g. rolling dice or playing "rock, paper, scissors"). Consider using PowerPoint karaoke for classroom warmups instead of a quiz! Games can be radical tools for learning and teaching.[14] In an educational setting, "peer learning through gamification"[15] works as a playified feedback method, where feedback is not given by the teacher but by peers whilst walking outdoors in pairs, asking each other questions about their (school) projects. The randomised draw of question and impulse cards helps shake things up.

Level 2:
Eating Mario's Mushrooms:
Tackle the Obstacles

Are you an avid gamer, a casual player, a curious bystander or an outspoken opponent? Do you view games as a "utopia" or as the "enemy" – which side will you take?

- You think games are a waste of time. [→ go to Theory]
  or
- You believe games can save the world. [→ go to Purpose]

Theory

Game studies, the academic discourse on games and play, distinguishes between two forms of play, *paidia* and *ludus.*[16] *Ludus* is a form of play strictly

Purpose

What are play and games for? Depending on the theoretical perspective (→ Theory), play is an important evolutionary mechanism for learning. We (humans

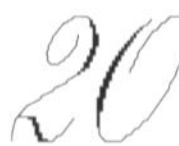

controlled by rules; *paidia* stands for the free form of play. These forms have four different distinctions that can be found in both *paidia* and *ludus: agon* (competition), *alea* (chance), *mimicry* (mimesis, role-playing) and *ilinx* (vertigo, loss of control). While gamification makes the most use of *ludus* as a the form and *agon* as a type, playification is more diverse and aims to cover the full range of play types and modes with a variety of game mechanics.[17] (→ go to Methods) Acceptance of the "magic circle" is key[18]: When we play, we create our own symbolic space, with its own rules and meanings. The knowledge that we are moving from "world x" to "world y", even if it's just for a short time, makes a difference: we're curious about the outcome, invite serendipity, are more open to experimentation, more willing try on a role because "it's just a game" – an alternate reality. Even in creating unnecessary obstacles[19] or submitting to the psychogeography of a city,[20] we explore play for different types of players (i.e. the explorer, the killer, the socializer, the achiever).[21]

and animals alike) learn through play. The perceived motivational and educational power of games has led to the development and funding of serious and applied games – games that serve a purpose other than entertainment. Gamification radicalises this in a behavioural way: we need to self-optimise! We count our daily steps to pay lower insurance rates; we earn a free coffee when we collect enough stamps; heavenly grace is ours when we confess our sins and pray the rosary; we study to get good grades. As early as 2010, Jesse Schell shared his "Visions of the Gamepocalypse", wherein every second of his life is somehow spent playing a game: for feedback, for a sense of progress, to promote his health or tackle challenges.[22] Playification opposes gamification! Play should not be used or exploited but, as Schiller's letters note, serve its own ends (→ go to Tutorial). Extrinsic motivation (points, badges, leaderboards) does not magically transform content into intrinsic motivation. On the contrary, rewards punish.[23]

Level 3:
Enlightenment:
I Can See Clearly Now The Rain Is Gone

Before we reach the bliss of play, the text oracle wants to put your belief system to the test:

- You do not believe you can invent your own games. [→ go to Methods]

or

- You believe playing games is (and should always be!) something for children only [→ go to Playgrounds]

Methods

You are about to be proven wrong: anyone can be a play designer! Here are some tips for inducing play and creating meaningful playful situations.[24]

- Play is voluntary by definition. Always bear in mind that there should be options for extroverts, introverts, and even non-participants.
- Introduce chance/*alea* (→ go to Theory) and unpredictability, e.g. by rolling dice, a wheel of fortune or any other randomiser used to turn things upside down.
- Change or break rules in existing games or structures for a sense of how the effect, feel, and dynamics change.
- Assign fictitious roles or flip roles, indulge in role play: swap between expert/teacher/mentor/student/noob/nerd/

Playgrounds

We can learn a lot from the approach of children and their playful view of the world. A rock can be a turtle; there are at least five ways to hold a spoon and countless strategies for avoiding bedtime. A "ludic attitude" can also make our adult lives more meaningful. (→ go to Definitions) The playgrounds are in art and music,[27] in education, across various media, materials and technologies. Consequently, "Digital play means not only forms of play generated by digital technologies, but also a creative practice, an innovative play with these technologies."[28] Projects of the "ludic society", such as their salons or installations, create subversive play, e.g. by playing Pong on a woman's dress,[29] whereas a higher education setting might explore "ludic the stranger – indulge in a reversed-roles classroom – “flip” the classroom![25]

- Explore, experiment, live a culture of error positivity. Invite unpredictability, even if it means (or because!) you as a facilitator will have to give up some of your power.
- See also PHEW (Play, Hybrid, Easy, Walkabout), an applied education framework.[26]

didactics” via playful interventions in Zoom meetings, or by inviting students and teachers on walkabouts.[30] Different learning types respond to different game and play mechanisms. (→ go to Theory) Playification uses multimodal, multi-sensory approaches that contextualise and de-contextualise challenge-based and analytical learning scenarios that are not focused on grades as outcome.[31]

Game Over – Or Shall We Have Another Go?

Playification seeks immersive closeness and aesthetic distance at once; it occupies the in-between space, dances in the play that is tender digitality. Become a “tender homo digitalis”[32] and take play seriously! And always with a smile.

The transformative power of play can help develop forward-thinking literacies[33], including shaping identities in physical, hybrid, and virtual spaces. It engenders agency in its fostering of creativity, leadership and resilience. When we create or participate in playful interventions, we build sustainable competencies for self-reflective systems.

This text invites you to reflect on your own playful agency. Thanks for playing! (→ go to Level 1)

1. Friedrich Schiller, *On the Aesthetic Education of Man in a Series of Letters,* ed. and trans. Elizabeth M. Wilkinson and L. A. Willoughby (Oxford: Clarendon Press), 107.
2. For more on this, see the research of Johanna Pirker, who has explored games and play around the world on her blog Johanna Pirker, accessed September 24, 2023, jpirker.com or the “gameZ & ruleZ” conference on non-human game mechanics, November 10–12, 2017, Walcheturm, Zurich, see gameZfestival, accessed September 24, 2023, www.gamezfestival.ch/2017

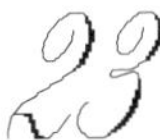

3. As beautifully illustrated in Oliver Brunko's images on the endpapers of this Volume.
4. Eric Zimmerman, *The Rules We Break: Lessons in Play, Thinking and Design* (New York: Princeton Architectural Press, 2022), 77.
5. "Gamification", Merriam-Webster, last updated September 7, 2023, www.merriam-webster.com/dictionary/gamification
6. See also Ivan Mosca, "+10! Gamification and deGamification", in *GAME: The Italian Journal of Game Studies,* no. 1 (2012): 77–89.
7. Alfie Kohn, *Punished by Rewards: The Trouble with Gold Stars, Incentive Plans, A's, Praise, and Other Bribes* (New York: Houghton Mifflin, 1993).
8. Matthias Flatscher, "Das Spiel der Kunst als die Kunst des Spiels: Bemerkungen zum Spiel bei Gadamer und Wittgenstein", in *Orte des Schönen: Phänomenologische Annäherungen,* ed. Reinhold Esterbauer (Würzburg: Königshausen & Neumann, 2003), 125–54; Katie Salen and Eric Zimmerman, *Rules of Play: Game Design Fundamentals* (Cambridge, MA: MIT Press, 2003).
9. Also called the ludic spirit, see Andrzej Marczewski, "The Ludic Spirit RAMP: Connecting Intrinsic Motivation to Playful Mindsets", Gamified UK, August 21, 2023, www.gamified.uk/category/ludic-spirit
10. For a critique of the current understanding and implementation of "gamification", see Mela Kocher, "Ludic Didactics: For an Inspired, Motivating and Playful Education", in *Games and Learning Alliance: 11th International Conference, GALA 2022, Tampere, Finland, November 30 – December 2, 2022, Proceedings,* ed. Kristian Kiili et al. (Cham: Springer, 2022), 193–201.
11. See Charlotte Axelsson and Mela Kocher, "Playful Times – Exploring World ... PHEW!", in *Changing Time – Shaping World: Changemaker in Arts & Education,* ed. Anna Maria Loffredo et al. (Bielefeld: transcript, 2022), 129–39.
12. Ideas for Games, developed by Beat Suter and Anja Fritsch from the GameLab at Zurich University of the Arts (ZHdK). See "GameLab", ZHdK, accessed September 24, 2023, gamelab.zhdk.ch/projects/ideasforgames
13. To name a few: "Random Emoji Generator", Perchance, accessed September 24, 2023, perchance.org/emoji; "Wheel of Names", Wheel of Names, accessed September 24, 2023, wheelofnames.com
14. Mela Kocher and René Bauer, "Spiele – radikale Lehr- und Lernmittel", *swissfuture: Magazin für Zukünfte* 20, no. 1 (2020): 26–29.
15. See "Educational Encounter", LeLa – LernLabor, accessed September 24, 2023, lela.ch/detail/produkte/ee02
16. Roger Caillois, *Les Jeux et les hommes: Le masque et le vertige* (Paris: Gallimard, 1958).
17. Beat Suter, Mela Kocher and René Bauer, eds., *Games and Rules: Game Mechanics for the "Magic Circle"* (Bielefeld: transcript, 2019).
18. Johan Huizinga, Homo Ludens: *A Study of the Play-Element in Culture* (London: Routledge, 1949).
19. Jane McGonigal, *Reality Is Broken: Why Games Make Us Better and How They Can Change the World* (New York: Penguin, 2011).
20. Guy Debord, "Theory of the Dérive", *Visual Culture: Critical Concepts in Media and Cultural Studies* 3 (1958): 77–81.
21. Take the Bartle Test here: "The Bartle Test of Gamer Psychology", Matthew Barr, accessed September 24, 2023, matthewbarr.co.uk/bartle
22. Jesse Schell, "Visions of the Gamepocalypse," The Long Now Foundation, July 27, 2010, longnow.org/seminars/02010/jul/27/visions-gamepocalypse
23. See Kohn, *Punished by Rewards.*
24. For a full explanation of play concepts and arguments, see Zimmerman, *The Rules We Break.*
25. Becki A. Brown, "Understanding the Flipped Classroom: Types, Uses and Reactions to a Modern and Evolving Pedagogy", *Culminating Projects in Teacher Development* 12 (2016): 1–26.
26. Axelsson and Kocher, "Playful Times".
27. For a discussion of playful approaches in Marcel Duchamp's readymades or John Cage's *Musicircus,* see Lily Díaz, "By Chance, Randomness and Indeterminacy Methods in Art and Design", *Journal of Visual Art Practice* 10, no. 1 (2011): 21–33.
28. Interview with Florian Faller, head of the "Digital Play" course at ZHdK, "Florian Faller, was bedeutet 'Digital Play'?", E-Learning, ZHdK, accessed September 25, 2023, elearning.zhdk.ch/community/florian-faller-was-bedeutet-digital-play-1
29. See Margarete Jahrmann and Max Moswitzer, Ludic Society, accessed September 25, 2023, ludic-society.net
30. Kocher, "Ludic Didactics".
31. Björn Nölte and Philippe Wampfler, *Schule ohne Noten: Neue Wege zum Umgang mit Lernen und Leistung* (Bern: hep, 2021).
32. See Charlotte Axelsson's article in this volume (page 4).
33. See also Axelsson and Kocher, "Playful Times".

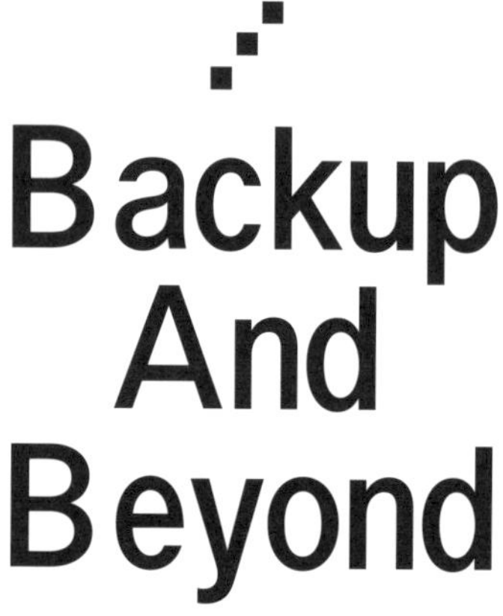

Backup And Beyond

Hannah Eßler engages theoretically and practically, both in her professional and personal life, with practices of archiving and the potential pitfalls of digitalisation. In her essay, she takes a narrative journey through the realms of digital and analogue memory, grappling with the question of how to cultivate and implement a thoughtful approach to managing one's own archive.

Hannah Eßler is studying in the MA Transdisciplinarity program and works as a freelance editor, researcher and author as well as in the E-Learning, Learning & Teaching Dossier of the Zurich University of the Arts.

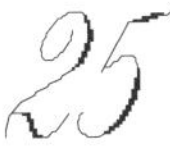

Moving

At the age of 80, my grandmother took a bold step. After living in the rented flat where my mother had grown up for 50 years, she, or rather my mother and I, began packing her belongings. During the move, she had to reduce her living space to about a quarter of its previous size. Yet she approached the task with pragmatism: after inspecting the new apartment and planning the furniture arrangement on paper, my grandmother systematically walked through the old one and pointed out the items she wanted to take with her. She had always had a sense of style, and among her many possessions, large and small, she seemed to know exactly which ones would continue to serve her needs and hold meaning for her in the future. Wheat was separated from the chaff. The "wheat", or good items, were carefully packed, transported and promptly arranged in their new home. Once the new home was deemed ready for occupancy, my grandmother resolutely closed the door to the old one behind her, never to return. Left behind were the possessions, now without purpose. They lacked history. My grandmother had taken it with her.

Because of the move, my grandmother took it upon herself to decide which items were worth keeping and which weren't. Her grandfather's attempts at composing fell victim to her downsizing, as did a great-aunt's collection of wartime recipes. She never asked about these things again. My mother and I were tasked with disposing of them. Some items we kept out of nostalgia, others out of curiosity or pragmatism. Some were taken in by neighbours and friends. The majority ended up at the dump, where we considered one last time where each item belonged: wood, glass, plastic, electronic waste, paper, metal. I personally delivered a folder of old letters back to my grandmother. Yes, this chapter is also part of your story. At first, she refused, but after a few weeks she asked for it back, and it has been lying in her cupboard ever since. I can still ask; she can still tell – or choose to remain silent. She has the power to give objects meaning or to take it away; she can change the meaning of things.

The objects that move us, that stir our emotions, are moved by us in turn. The significance of our memories lies not only in the memories themselves, but also in the fact that we carry them with us throughout our lives. The challenge of moving is not so much the lifting of boxes as it is the questioning of each individual item as to its place in the new environment. What do I leave behind? What do I give away? What do I choose to surround myself with? Moving reminds me of the responsibility I have towards these objects: to move them, to allow them to move me, to care for them, to give them away or dispose of them.

Questions in place of morals: How do I inhabit the digital realm? How do I arrange my digital space, and how often have I moved within it? Who will eventually take on the task of cleaning out my digital abode?

Losing

Around nine o'clock in the morning on 11 May 2023, I was sitting at my desk in my room, staring at my computer screen. The text input had stopped responding to my keystrokes. For a moment, time seemed to stand still, then the screen went dark. When I pressed the power button, it hesitated for a moment before glowing a light grey – and displaying a simple graphic: a folder with a question mark. The meaning of this symbol began to sink in. It meant that the computer's internal hard drive had stopped communicating with the rest of the machine. The computer was experiencing an acute and total loss of memory. There had been no fall, no spillage of tea – externally there was no cause and no trace of what had happened. Nevertheless, in one fell swoop, all my data had disappeared.

The silent shock of this event reverberated through me on several levels. Firstly, it upheaved my plans for the coming weeks. Procuring a new computer, setting up accounts, and installing software became the urgent tasks at hand. My initial optimism about attempting data recovery dissipated quickly – the associated costs often soared into the four-figure range, with no certainty about what they might unearth: would it be the meticulously structured Word document containing notes for my Master's thesis, or just remnants of old files from some forgotten programme? Even so, I remained uncertain about the extent of my loss. Hadn't I, at some point, sent many things via email? Uploaded them to a drive? Printed copies? The hard drive, a discreet object no larger than the palm of my hand, seemed to span an unfathomable expanse, and I embarked on a systematic inventory of my losses. The realisation seeped into consciousness only gradually.

“ […]
to move them
↘
to allow them
to move me
↙
to care for them
⁂
to give them away
→
or dispose them
↓

I found myself in a situation similar to my grandmother's: it wasn't just the computer; even my own memory seemed to have suffered from data loss. I had never felt disoriented so often whilst out on the streets before. I had lost my composure; the familiar routines of my everyday life had been disrupted. My reaction was close to panic: within days, I had subscribed to a cloud service and cast aside all my reservations about tech giants, data behemoths, and subscription models. One prevailing thought consumed me: I won't let this happen again. Consequently, I embarked on a determined journey through my digital and physical storage spaces, with the aim of gathering everything worth preserving in my newly acquired (non) location. I uncovered seven cloud accounts and drives, five active email addresses, two old hard drives, a handful of USB sticks, and the occasional download link. Some items I had thought were lost miraculously resurfaced. Above all, I stumbled upon boundless gigabytes of music I never listen to, photos I never peruse, and PDFs of texts I've never read. Half-finished writing projects, a quirky collection of screenshots, a tangle of unnamed audio recordings, outdated backups – in short, it was as if I had opened a concealed attic hatch, and I now gazed in amazement and mild bewilderment at the long-forgotten fragments of the past. Whilst the act of physical relocation repeatedly reminded me of the weight and volume of my analogue possessions, in the digital realm I seemed boundless, leading to an immeasurable inventory. The trend towards tiny houses, sustainability, and minimalism finds no equivalent here. The illusion of boundless space, limitless data and ever-cheaper storage capacity tempts us to save everything (and multiple copies of it) without restraint. That is, until the digital infrastructure falters and its full impact dawns on the consciousness.

The guilt I felt as I sifted through those dusty mountains of data was accompanied by the realisation that without the hard drive crash I probably wouldn't have crossed those digital thresholds for years, if not decades. So, this single loss unexpectedly restored to me an immeasurable trove of almost forgotten treasures. And while I am still hesitating whether and how to revive certain lost texts on paper or in Word, or whether to consign them to oblivion, all the other files are emerging from their obsolete

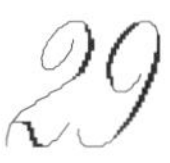

storage formats. After years of neglect, they now insist on the care they deserve.

Questions in place of morals: Do we determine what we want to remember in the digital realm and what we don't? What have I lost without even noticing? What do I retain without realising it? What do the items I keep, forget, lose, or discard reveal about me? What do I store where, what do I keep multiple copies of, what do I delete?

Telling

It's August and I'm back at the same desk, working on my Master's thesis. Actually, I'm at three desks at once: on the analogue one, there's a pile of notes, pens, a bowl of nuts, a photo and a selection of books from various libraries; on the digital one is a folder system housing photos, screenshots, text documents, and PDFs. My citation programme is open, as is my Notes app; in the browser I have search engines, databases, library catalogues, and a handful of other websites at my disposal. But it's at my mental desk that the real work happens; it's here that I piece together the disparate materials from the other two desks, that I weave them into a coherent narrative.

My digital workspace is gaining weight. The wealth of possibilities it offers can easily lead me to overlook what doesn't fit on it: everything that hasn't been flattened[1] – either because it doesn't fit the digital format or because it hasn't been deemed significant. My work only enriches the digital realm when I think both within and beyond its boundaries. Rather than seeing digital and analogue as antithetical or mutually exclusive, I explore their interconnectedness.

These questions become apparent when considered within the dimensions of space (What analogue locations house digital data and with what political structures are they imbued?[2]) and time (How do we respond to the increasingly short lifespan of storage media,[3] coupled with the rapid growth of data volumes and the rapid evolution of media and formats?). I want to bridge these dimensions through the lens of practicality: how do we organise, select, use, and maintain our personal archives? A tender approach doesn't necessarily require new management tools, disc cleaning programmes, unlimited storage space, or information leaflets. On the contrary, it requires our most precious resource: our attention. It involves more

“ […]
what connections
--
do I draw between my
physical,
mental
/
and digital
storage spaces?
⁑

than just mastering and replicating routines; it involves acquiring a specific sensitivity that is worthy of what we hold dear. When we support each other in cultivating such a practice, it can be as binding as it is bonding.

The challenge that my digital workspace presents to me – not only in my Master's thesis – is to ensure that I do not lose sight of my subject. On the other hand, digital perspectives can also bring it into sharper focus. For example, the excitement surrounding new tools like ChatGPT offers an opportunity to recognise that as "narrating monkeys"[4] we should not leave history/ies to its/their own device. This is a responsibility, a task, but also a realm of possibility.[5] We can tell a story with each "thing", but not the same story with each one. By tending to our digital and analogue archives, we inscribe the history of objects, rewriting, reimagining, and reframing them, thereby writing our own history with and through them.

Questions in place of morals: What connections do I draw between my physical, mental and digital storage spaces? How much value do I place on the preservation of my data? How do digital archives reshape the epistemic practices of collecting, organising and archiving? How can and do we want to transform these practices – and how do they transform us?

1. The "cultural technique of flattening" is extensively addressed by Sybille Krämer in various lectures as well as in Sybille Krämer, *Figuration, Anschauung, Erkenntnis: Grundlinien einer Diagrammatologie* (Berlin: Suhrkamp, 2016).
2. I don't necessarily have to adopt Kittler's polemics in this regard. See Friedrich Kittler, "There Is No Software", in *The Truth of the Technological World: Essays on the Genealogy of Presence,* trans. Erik Butler (Redwood City: Stanford University Press, 2014), 219–29.
3. The German Research Foundation (DFG) currently recommends a ten-year period for "long-term archiving". See DFG, "Guidelines for Safeguarding Good Research Practice", 20 last modified on April 20, 2022, zenodo.org/records/6472827
4. Samira El Ouassil and Friedemann Karig, *Erzählende Affen: Mythen, Lügen, Utopie. Wie Geschichten unser Leben bestimmen* (Berlin: Ullstein, 2021).
5. "You can create art and beauty on a computer". See "Hacker Ethics", Chaos Computer Club, accessed September 3, 2023, www.ccc.de/en/hackerethics

Can You Hear It Splashing?

All around us it flows. The floor, the walls, even the air is full of rushing currents. Beautiful zeros and ones, ones and zeros. If you listen carefully, you will notice that the quiet splashing has long since turned into something else. Marcial Koch takes us on a dive trip: an AR sound experience.

Marcial Koch is an interaction designer, teaches Human Computer Interaction in the E-Learning, Learning & Teaching Dossier of the Zurich University of the Arts and studies scenography at the University of Applied Sciences and Arts Northwestern Switzerland

With their permission, this work includes additional sounds from the Youtubers RAIACAD0564 and lAMNOTGOOMBA. Follow the instructions below to get started:

1 – Find a place where you won't disturb anyone, as the experience includes sound through speakers.
2 – Take out your smartphone, unmute it and set the volume to maximum.
3 – Scan the QR code and visit the following website:

4 – Allow the website to access your camera and to your device motion sensors.
5 – If you receive an error message and the camera screen is not displayed, check the website settings of your current browser and allow the camera.
6 – Click the "Let it babble!" button.
7 – Scan the ARTag below to test.
8 – Have fun!

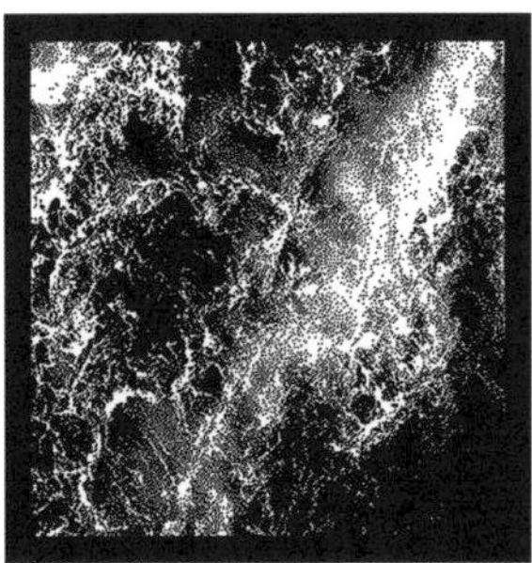

[year] – [Transition time of 3.4 Mb = modern smartphone image]
We are devouring data ever more voraciously. We thirst for more, faster. A bit became a billion. A drop has become an ocean.

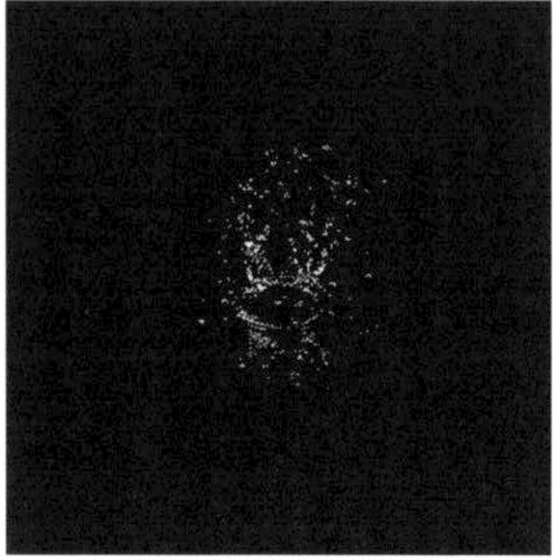

1962 – 25 h
It all starts with a single drop. AT&T's Bell 103 is the first commercial dial-up modem, transmitting data at a speed of 300 bits per second (bps) over the telephone landline.

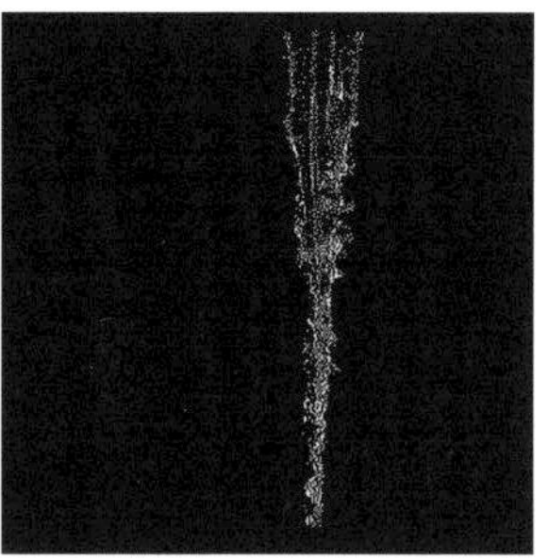

1973 – 6.25 h
Several drops form a small trickle. The VA3400 dial-up modem quadruples the speed to 1,200 bps.

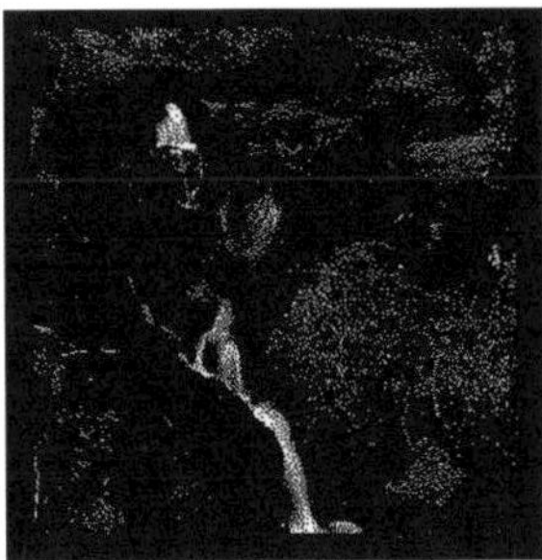

1984 – 47 min

Trickles flow together to form a slow-wmoving stream rivulet. With the creation of the V.22bis transmission standard, speeds of 2,400 bps become commonplace. Later that year, V.32 is released with a speed of 9,600 bps, leading to the development of the digital fax.

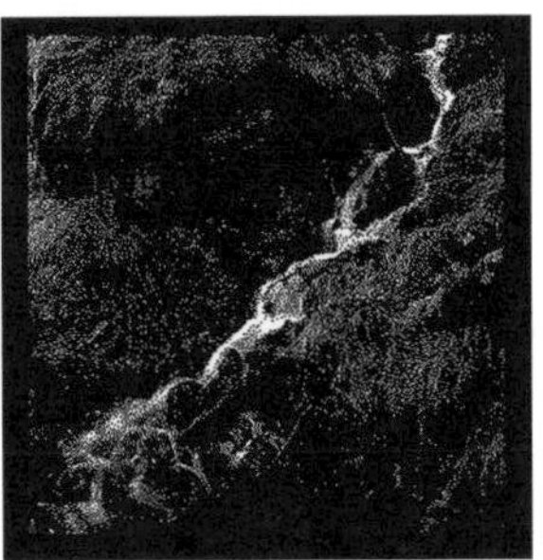

1991 – 31 min

Small raindrops start to fall from the sky until the rivulet bed becomes a regular brook. The mobile phone network overtakes its analogue technology counterparts when the second generation, 2G, is launched in Finland, enabling speeds of 9,600 bps. At the same time, the V.32bis dial-up transmission is standardised at 14,400 bps (14.4 kilobits per second, Kbps).

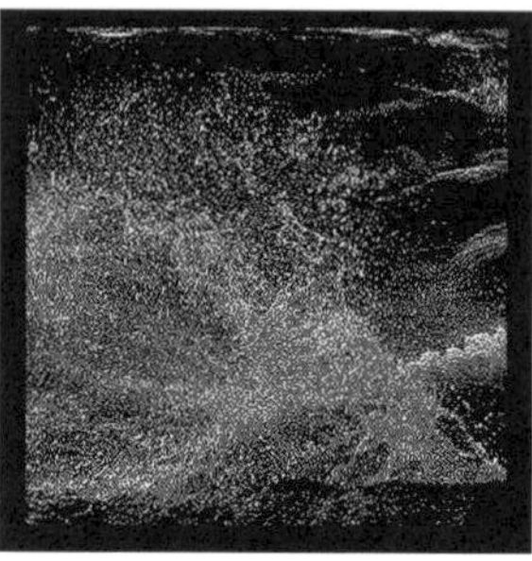

1991

With the opening of the World Wide Web (WWW) to the general public, swarms of data begin to emerge. Trickle sounds are starting to be heard everywhere. The merging of trickles means there is no longer just a downstream flow, but flow in all directions.

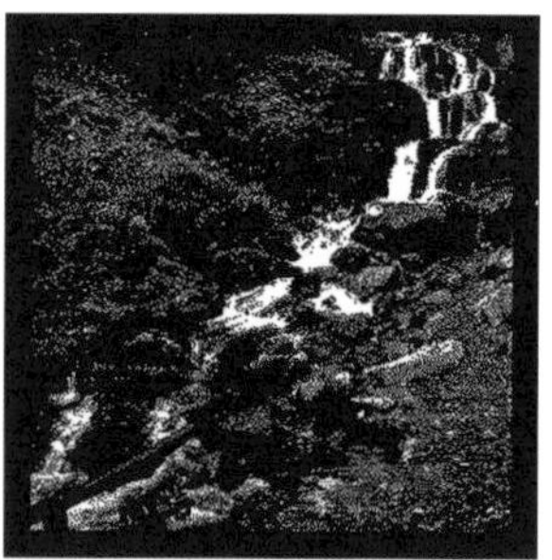

1994 – 15.5 min

Brooks converge, creating the first narrow streams. With the advent of the World Wide Web, the world thirsts for advanced technologies to cope with the swarms of digital data. The V.34 dial-up standard enables data flow at 28.8 Kbps.

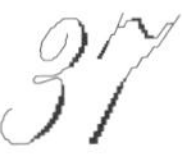

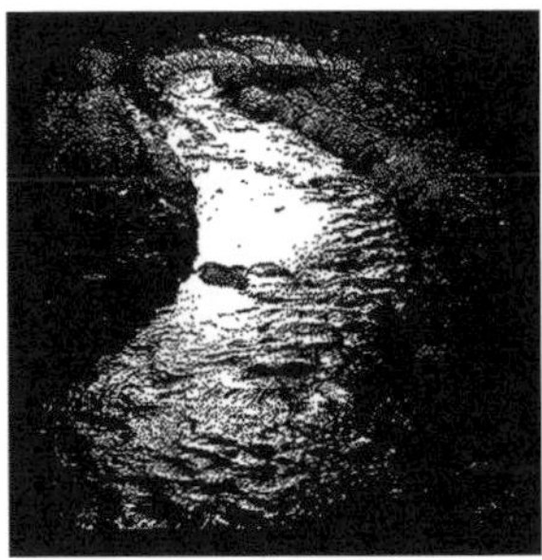

1996 – 8 min

Streams continue to swell until the water is suddenly up to your knees. The era of dial-up modems peaks at 56 Kbps.

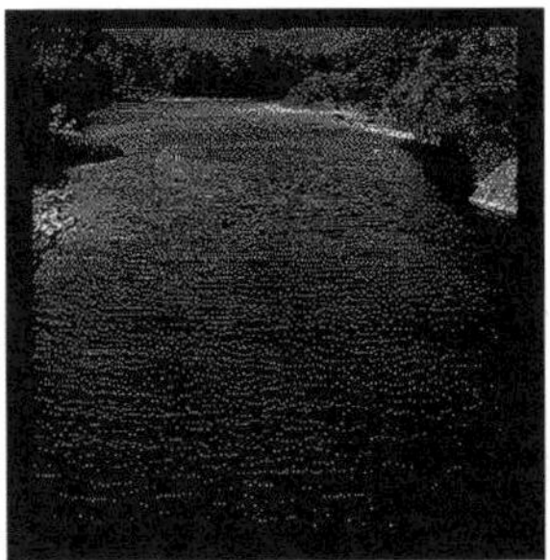

1998 – 27 sec

Hold on tight or you will be swept away by the current. The masses of water turn the stream into a river. The sound of dial-up modems disappears, giving way to an era of broadband technologies such as the digital subscriber line (DSL), asymmetric digital subscriber line (ADSL), and cable modems. Before long, 1,000 Kbps (1 megabits per second, Mbps) is commonly available.

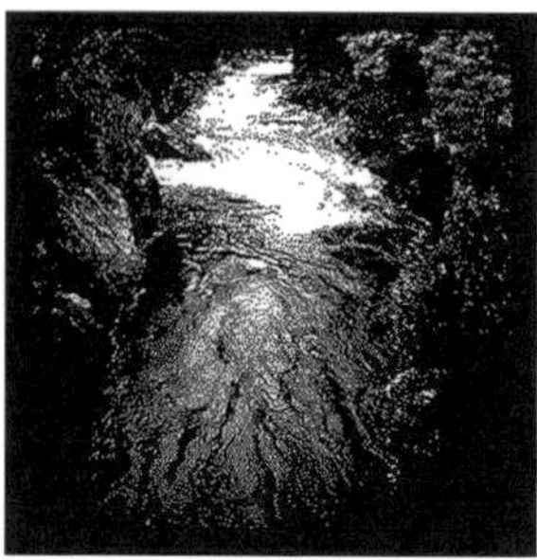

2001 – 2.45 sec

A moderate rain pelts us mercilessly. We are surrounded by water, it is impossible not to get wet. The introduction of the Apple Airport marks the commercial breakthrough of wireless LAN (WLAN). Protocols for this had been standardised as early as the late 1990s under the name Wi-Fi. Private households can now connect to the WWW wirelessly at speeds of up to 11 Mbps. At the same time, the 3G mobile network – with speeds of around 200 Kbps – appears on the horizon.

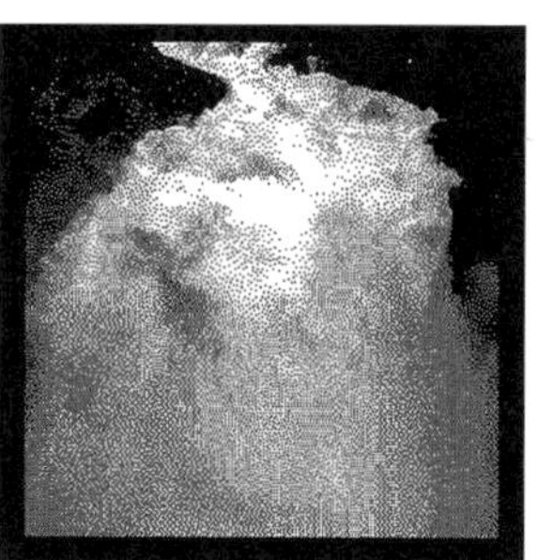

2009 – 0.27 sec

Heavy rain falls. The river becomes so torrential that attempting to cross it would result in immediate drowning. Wi-Fi is omnipresent. The release of the new Wi-Fi 4 protocol allows speeds of up to 72 Mbps, while cable companies offer broadband of up to 100 Mbps.

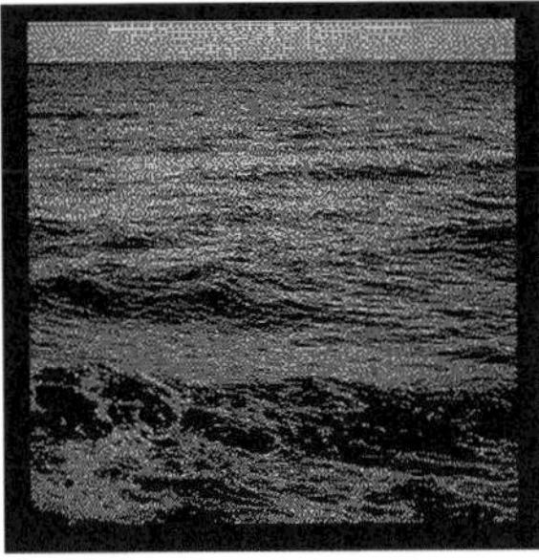

2023 – 0.002 sec

The rain seems to have no end. All the water from the rivers forms an ocean. Higher and lower waves come from all directions. We now find ourselves on the 5G mobile network, promising speeds of 1,000 Mbps (1 gigabits per second, Gbps) to 10 Gbps. Fibre-to-the-home (FTTH) technology in private households offers speeds of up to 10 Gbps.

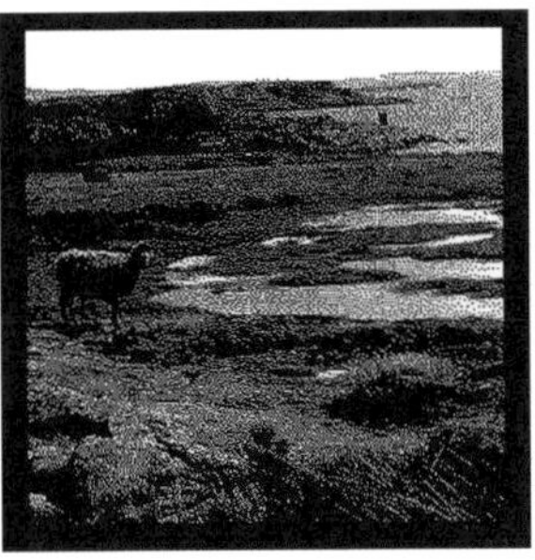

2023

And still, we cry out for more. Isn't the ocean enough? We've been drowning for a while now; it's just that we've grown used to the feeling. Test labs in Japan have already reached transmission speeds of 319,000 Gbps (319 terrabits per second, Tbps).

Dance Score Weave

Friederike Lampert describes her teaching method in this visual essay, which shows the process by which students use the technique she developed with the Mecaniques from a creative and cultural praxis for the planning and structuring of choreography. A moving interweaving – what it means to aesthetically weave bodies, one digital, the other analogue. All together now – let's dance.

Friederike Lampert is professor of choreography for the Master's programme in Dance at Zurich University of the Arts.

In the spring of 2023, I taught a choreography course to students persuing a Master's degree in Dance. The course was called "Lines: On Notation and Scores". The idea was to inspire and confront the students with creative methods, especially from other artistic and cultural fields, which they were to use as inspiration for preparing or annotating a choreographic process / work. Drawing on the book *Lines* by Tim Ingold, in which the anthropologist presents an anthropological archeology of the line, we researched notation and scores from various cultural fields (writing, music, dance, calligraphy, fabrics, architecture, genealogy, urban planning, agriculture, and so on) and handicrafts (drawing, writing, mapping, etching, weaving, etc.).[1] We looked more closely at keyboard art and practiced it either as dance score or in the form of expanded choreography work. We reflected on various dance notation methods and dance score writing throughout history. At the heart of the course was an assignment to weave a dance score and explain and show how the embodiment of the woven dance score might look. The aim was to step out of the familiar and into new creative processes of dance making.

"What do walking, weaving, observing, storytelling, singing, drawing and writing have in common? The answer is that they all proceed along lines",[2] Tim Ingold notes. Although his book only mentions dance and choreography in passing, it is very clear that the practice of choreography can be prominently applied to the narration of *lines*. Choreography understood as *ars combinatoria* – the varied combination of movements in time and space – can be read as a complex meshwork of lines on different levels: lines in the shape of bodies, materials, or objects; the lines that trace movement in space; imaginary lines in connection to space; the lines of space in motion; the lines in dance or music writing (notations, scores, annotations), and so on.

Regarding the lines in dance notation, I would like to distinguish between two different uses of notation:

Score:
A tool / method for preparation, the act of composing (dance), happens *before* performing the piece. Can be regarded as an independent artwork.

Annotation:
A tool/method for analysis, reflection, and documentation, happens *after* performing the piece. Can be regarded as an independent artwork.

Keyboard Art
In the course we focused on the creation of scores. Usually, the choreographer uses individual writing on paper or on the computer to prepare and collect ideas for a choreographed piece (notes, sketches, drawings). This can then be used as a score to create the choreographed work in the studio or (when performing improvised dance) live on stage. The creation of the score is already an act of choreography, built through the combination of the elements to be "written". In one exercise we took inspiration from the interdisciplinary artist Pelenakeke Brown, who transformed woven patterns via lines (letters/numbers, symbols) created using a keyboard.[3] The process of composing with lines found on a computer keyboard led to new insights into how space, directions, counterpoint and pattern come together in a choreographer's mind. The use of computers offered rich possibilities for creativity, and it yielded beautiful results:[4]

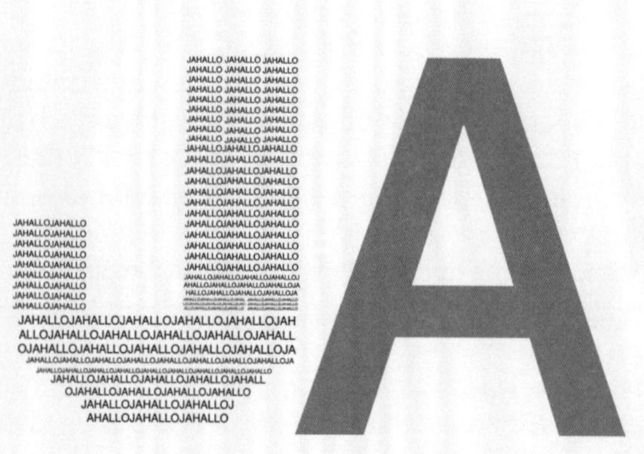

Dance Score Weave

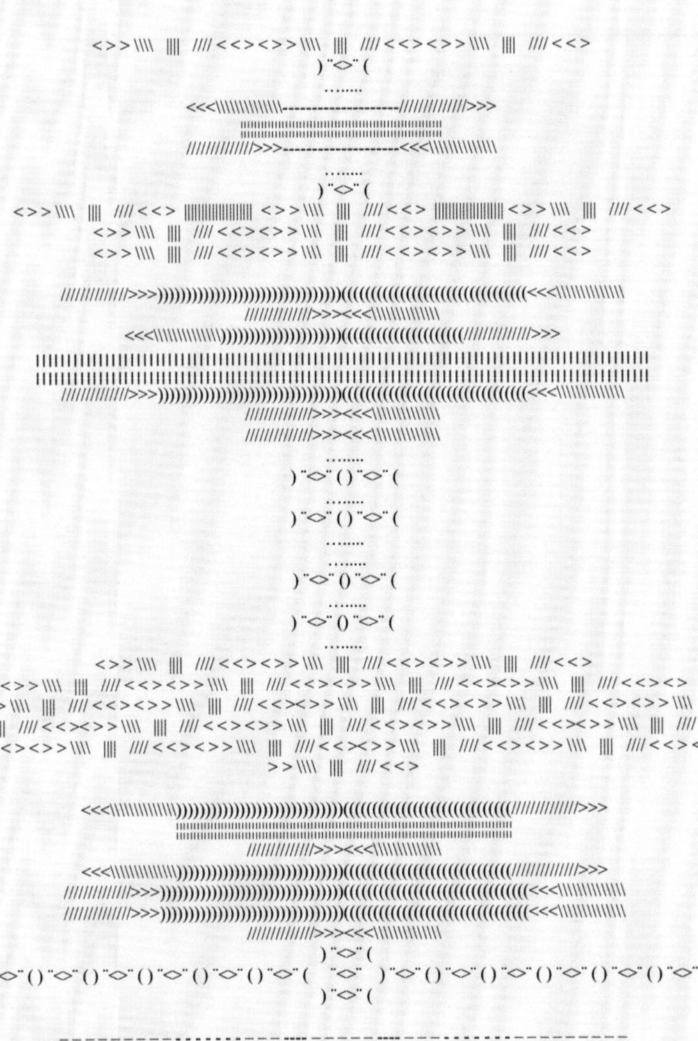

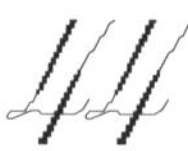

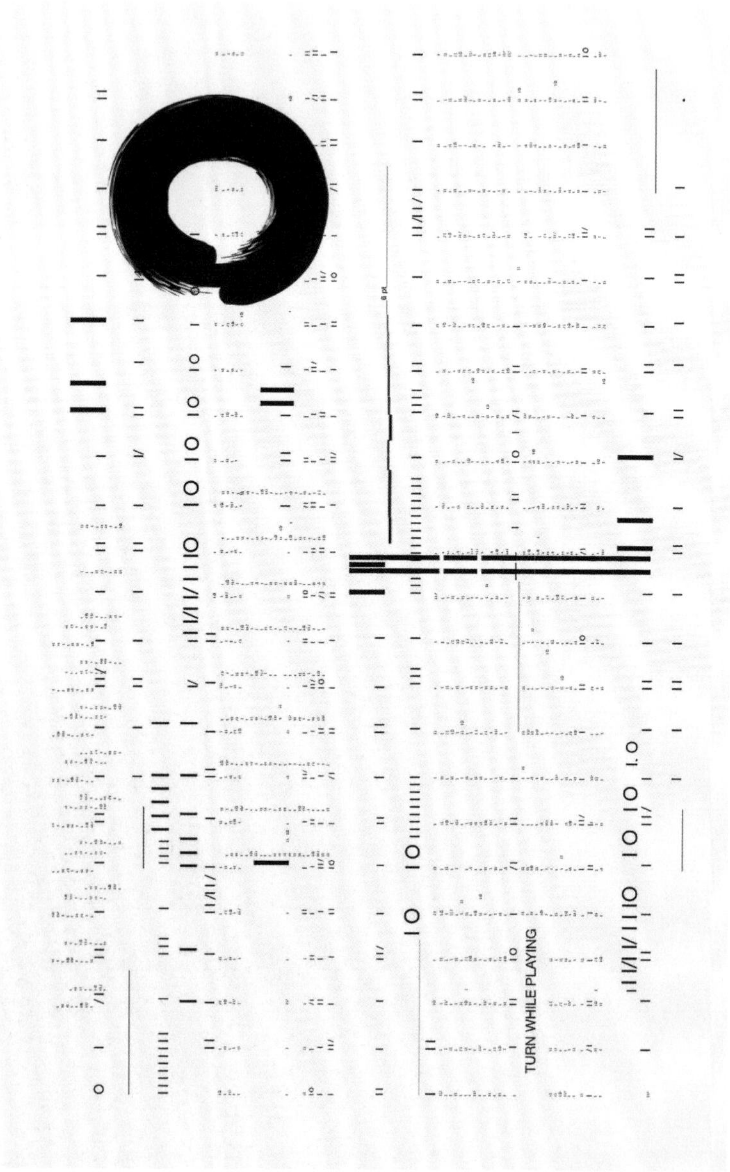

TURN WHILE PLAYING

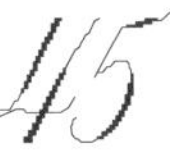


```
........-----

        ..............----------@@@@@@@@@@++++++++++..................------

 .
       .
            .
 .       .       ..........       7777777777777777000000000000000000000000000000000000000000
                            .       77777777777777000000000000100000000010000000000000010
                          ....       777777777777010000000000100111111111111111111000010
                           ...       77777777777100000100001011111111111111111111000010
                            ..       777777777010000100001001111111111111111110000010
                             .       7777777000000000050100111111111111111110000010
                                      777777000000000900100011111111111111100000000
                                       77777000000000900100001111111111111100000001
                                        7777000000000100100001111111111111100000010
                                         777000000900101000011111111111110000000
                                          77000500100100000001111111111111000000
                                          7700000000101000000011111111110000000
                                         77111111011100000000011111111110000000
                                        7711111111101000000000001111111100000001
                                       77111111101100000000000011111110000100
                                       711111101100000000000000011110000001
                                       (1111777777000001100000000001100000010
                                        ) 7777777000001110000000000001000011
                                        ( 777777000001111000000000001100001
                                         ) 77771000001111100000000000001000
                                         7177700000111111100000000000101
                                          717700000111111111000000000111
                                           717—000111111111100000000011
                                            )7700001111111111111000001
                                            (70000111111111111110001
                                             (00001111111111111111101
                                              ||0000111111000001100 1
                                                0001111110000000111
                                                  01111000000011
```

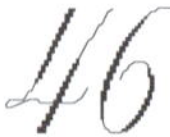

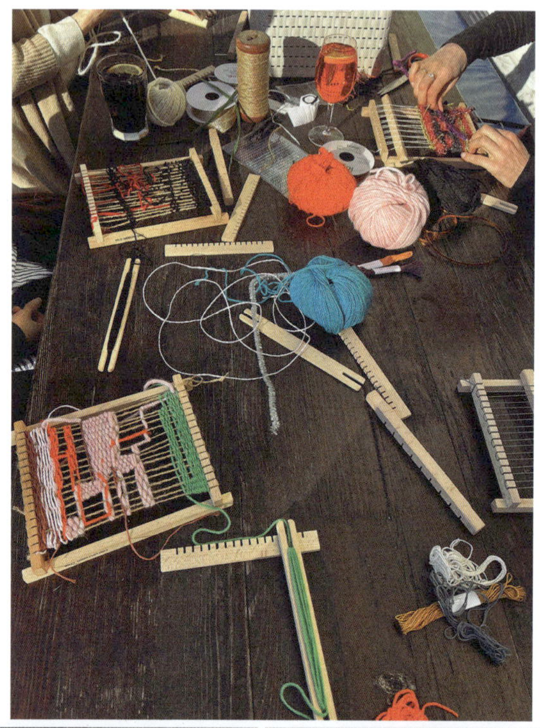

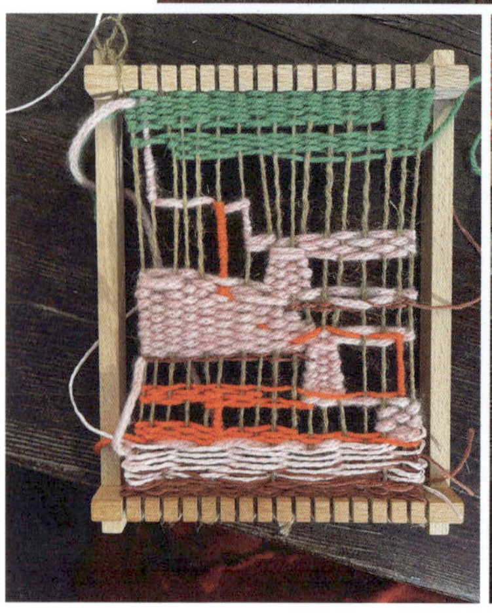

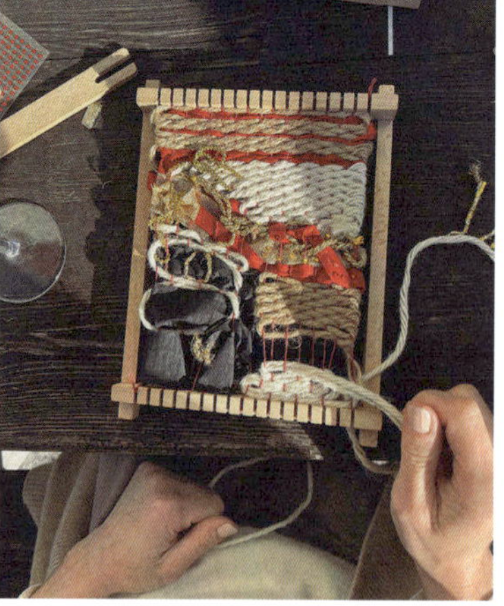

Weaving

After working with the digital, we moved on to the analogue: creating a score by weaving.

I gave a brief introduction to weaving techniques and the work of textile artists such as Anni Albers and Sheila Hicks. The students worked on creating woven scores with different types of yarn, string, and other materials using little table looms.

The task was:

- Weave a dance score.
- Work on the score – think of a performative translation of the "lines" you see.
- Present and explain how you would perform the woven score.

Tender connections

Every *line* creates a connection – whether made from analogue materials or assembled from digital lines on a computer screen. The resulting pattern or texture is a transformation of the thoughtful, tender act of (inter)weaving and composing.

1. Further sources of ideas for this course included Bojana Kunst, "On the Threads and Knots of Practice: Choreography and Weaving", in *Choreographie als Kulturtechnik,* ed. Sabine Huschka and Gerald Siegmund (Berlin: Neofelis, 2022), 235–51; the concept of string figures from Donna Haraway, *Staying with the Trouble: Making Kin in the Chthulucene* (Durham, NC: Duke University Press, 2016); and the performance *Fäden,* chor. Ivana Müller, Therese-Giehse-Halle, Münchner Kammerspiele, Munich, November 25, 2021.
2. Tim Ingold, Lines: *A Brief History* (London: Routledge 2007), 1.
3. "A Traveling Practice", Pelenakeke Brown, accessed September 18, 2023, kekebrown.com/a-traveling-practice
4. Works by course participants (MA Dance students at the Zurich University of the Arts).

Oliver Ruf

Tactile Media

On a search for connections and a mission to sound out the spaces in between, Oliver Ruf embarks on a linguistic scavenger hunt through the histories and gestures of specific terms. At the end: a tentative click, a gentle touch, a stumble.

Oliver Ruf is Research Professor of Communication Aesthetics at Bonn-Rhine-Sieg University of Applied Sciences.

I.

The thrust of the explanation of media communication attempted here is that sensuality is at least culturally and discursively related to that which we refer to as sensitivity or sensibility *(Empfindsamkeit),* i.e., the designation of an emotional and affective state once known as *tendresse amoureuse* (= tender love).[1] Its background is specifically that of the courtly gallantry that historically fostered a lingering, sentimental culture of emotion – one that even led to the creation and charting of an imaginary land its topography in the form of a *carte de tendre,* or *Map of Tendre.* The central route on this very real, indeed very material map (which works like an interface), literally embodies Tenderness, a path that runs far afield from enmity and all-too-perilous, unbridled passion.[2] Tenderness can thus be understood as a highly empathic form of behavioural regulation, as an expression of emotional community and an ideal of love. At the same time, however, tenderness remains a concept that acts as a medium, particularly in the search for one's own identity and in measuring oneself against others (within that community). A closer look at the etymology of the term sheds further light on the direction in which this discourse is heading. The Middle High German word *zarten* – the stem of the word that forms the modern-day German term *Zärtlichkeit,* or tenderness – means "to caress", which points to the fact that tenderness in the Middle Ages was understood more in terms of a sensation-based perception of hidden connections, as the perception of the invisible. Tenderness is, therefore, fundamentally close to that which could be at the very least be subsumed under the dispositif of a certain aesthetic; *zart* can be considered as the barely perceptible qualities of a work. In that case, tenderness also encompasses a delicacy, or sensitivity *(Zartgefühl),* a newfound receptivity to the nature or disposition of certain qualities, such as the beauty of a work of art. But even from this perspective, tenderness remains a category of emotion. Art should ultimately, as they say, not only be beautiful, but should, above all, move the hearts of its audience, as if a sensitive experience were woven into the very fabric of art, or as if feeling itself were an aesthetic principle. Tenderness blends such percepts, characterised by their sweetness and strength (today we might even say their *cuteness)*[3], although it can also be disturbing (confusing, giving rise to feelings of uncertainty, and so on).

It is at this point that tender media come into play in a very concrete (= media-practical) way, namely by their gestural[4] and tactile characteristics. Tender media, in the context of the briefly mentioned history of the concept of tenderness, can be seen as tools for uncovering the unseen, rooted in their tactile nature where touch is always implied. These media, in a way, touch upon or elicit *(rühren)* beauty from the concealed – and, as a gesture, tenderly and distinctly disrupt by revealing the often imperceptible qualities of, for instance, a work of art. Tender gestures primarily arise from natural, tactile interactions, predominantly involving bodily movements, particularly those of the hands and fingers, which are closely connected to a message.[5] In the context of digital discourse, recent developments have shown that the recognition of gestures by technical systems is significantly improved when tactile feedback is integrated.[6] Here, individuals involved in human-system interactions are fully aware that they are interacting with a machine. Furthermore, when hardware imposes mechanical or logical constraints on gestural movements, users generally accept these constraints as essential requirements.[7] The primary aim of these tender gestures is usually to manipulate visual elements such as buttons and menus. The underlying goal is always to create an efficient interface. The challenge lies, for example, in the *tap-and-hold* requirement, a seemingly simple gesture that opens the door to a wide range of different interactions. However, users need to learn which specific elements this gesture affects, a learning process that can be aided by textual labels, among other methods.[8] Object-oriented gestures, by contrast, are more unambiguous because they establish a clear link between the object being manipulated and the intended interaction. The greater the number of gestures involved, the more expansive the machine's gestural vocabulary. That vocabulary can be reduced through contextual reuse of gestures, where available options are adjusted based on the user's context of use. This may involve continuously visualising the system's status for the user or physically separating different interactions using tangible representations.[9]

II.

Tender gestures can, accordingly, be classified both in media theory and in media practice through the concepts of semantics, functionality, and description: the semantics of a gesture describe its meaning, the content of the message it conveys and its intended purpose. Functionality, on the other hand, describes what the gesture does within the interface, while the description of a gesture outlines its spatial and temporal execution. Command gestures activate system functions such as closing or undoing actions. Indicator gestures direct attention to specific elements within the user's environment. Manipulative gestures allow for the manipulation or modification of the data space. These two categories of gestures are closely related as they both involve modifying elements of the perceptual space. Control gestures replicate or imitate specific actions or behaviours.[10] All of these media gestures, particularly the tender ones, possess a distinct start and end direction. Changes in direction, speed, and acceleration also play a role in the message and recognition of a gesture. For instance, circular movements are employed in rotating and scrolling controls, the functions of which are often based on the concept of an unlimited number of revolutions.[11] Regardless of the specific focus of gestural control, one thing is clear: all these implications of gesture – whether centred on a physical gesture alone (such as hand movements) or explicitly tied to digital interfaces – revolve around the concept of tactility in general and, more specifically, the tactility of tenderness. Reflecting on these gestures involves addressing both technical requirements and sensory connotations. Jean-Luc Nancy spoke of "a gesture toward *touching* upon *sense*",[12] highlighting the privileged role of their tactile dimension, the act of touching. To Nancy's mind, touch serves as a sensory heuristic across media of a bodily and non-bodily nature, acting as a method for initiating provisional connections with objects; it is only through touching and feeling our way that we gain a sensory understanding of our environment, that we establish adaptive relationships.[13] Nancy places focus on the tactile, the haptic and the sense of touch, as these evoke different modes of knowledge generation and perception that ultimately converge on mediality as a form of contact: "This touch is infinitely indirect, deferred – machines, vehicles, photocopies, eyes, still other hands are all interposed – but it continues as a slight, resistant, fine texture, the infinitesimal dust of a contact, anywhere interrupted and pursued."[14] The establishment of contact, emblematic of communication itself, occurs through touch and can have a tender quality, whether this touch occurs directly between individuals, or – as in a situation of digitality – between people via machines, or in the interaction between people and the machines themselves.

III.

One example of what might be called a medial-tender, digital communication scenario is what one might refer to as the act of pressing a button. Buttons on digital devices are, in essence, constantly being caressed,[15] as each button press requires the user to make a decision. However, because of the limited range of choices typically available, pressing a button isn't really a choice in the traditional sense. At the same time, media history shows that the act of pressing a button has played a significant role in stabilising the principle of written communication. The button affects both the medium and the human user, but remains physically separate from them. Is the button a medium in its own right or does it simply belong to a medium – is it a device? It is a media tool, of a tender nature, without which digital media would often cease to function effectively. In this context, the sense of sight divides the world into what the gaze focuses on directly and what lies at the periphery of the field of vision. This creates a division between haptic and visual feedback. While the eyes perceive the results of a keystroke (on a computer keyboard, for example), tactile sensations often fade into the background, as if the act of a keystroke were metaphorically taking place behind the screen.[16] In this way, the act of pressing a button operates both internally and externally, capable of either disrupting or benefiting the system. Consequently, the button places the human being in the paradoxical situation of entering from both outside and inside. In interpretations found within the history of theories related to tactility and gesture (such as those by Marshall McLuhan and Vilém Flusser),[17] the eradication of the button press enables a more holistic perception, but it can also introduce a form of interference. In reality, a complex dynamic emerges, characterised by the tension between the illusion that pressing a button reveals the essence of the machine and the intricate, impenetrable web of nested lists within

/

Buttons
on digital devices
are
[.·]
constantly
being
⁂
caressed
⁑

lists. Add to this the fact that once a button is pressed, it sets off a cascade of decisions that can no longer be stopped: media tenderness to infinity.

The fascination of the button push touches upon the rational principle of cause and effect, coupled with the immediate accessibility of the medium. Consequently, the fact that buttons are ever multiplying comes as no surprise. Buttons provide access to spaces, as does the click of a button in a computer browser. That causality is illusionary becomes apparent when one realises that the button consolidates the complexity of the computer's internal processes; the cause of the interaction shifts to precede the effect and is ultimately lost within the circuitry. Pressing a button becomes a choice, albeit not a real decision. The power button becomes an invitation for input, and the output – an emotional trigger – becomes the effect of an emotion-laden (tactile-tender) initiation of contact.

However, all of these phenomena occur predominantly in the context of practical media use,[18] primarily to serve individual communication needs. Tender media are always essentially utilitarian. However, they are also emotional media and, as such, transformative media.[19] And they are – perhaps inherently – digital media, or at least a consequence of the significant influence of media technology on human communicative sensibility. This influence obviously leads to a pronounced emotionalisation: pointedly at the intersection of the *Realm of the Senses* and the *Realm of Perception.*[21]

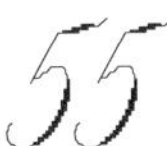

1. See overall Burkhard Meyer-Sickendiek, *Zärtlichkeit: Höfische Galanterie als Ursprung der bürgerlichen Empfindsamkeit* (Munich: Wilhelm Fink, 2016), 12.
2. See ibid., 16.
3. See Annekathrin Kohut, ed., “Cuteness: Das Niedliche als ästhetische Kategorie”, special issue, *Kunstforum International* 289 (2023).
4. See Oliver Ruf, “Zur Geste der Medien”, in *Epistemologien der Geste: Körper, Medien, Künste,* ed. Luca Viglialoro and Johannes Wassmer (Berlin: De Gruyter, 2023), 75–91.
5. See Justine Cassell, “A Framework for Gesture Generation and Interpretation”, in *Computer Vision for Human-Machine Interaction,* ed. Roberto Cipolla and Alex Pentland (New York: Cambridge University Press, 1998), 191–215, here 193.
6. See Nikolaos G. Tsagarakis et al., “Haptic-Enabled Multimodal Interface for the Planning of Hip Arthroplasty”, *IEEE Mutimedia* 13, no. 3 (2006): 40–48.
7. See Rainer Dorau, *Emotionales Interaktionsdesign: Gesten und Mimik interaktiver Systeme* (Heidelberg: Springer, 2011), 38.
8. See ibid., 115.
9. See Philip Kortum, ed., *HCI beyond the GUI: Design for Haptic, Speech, Olfactory, and Other Nontradtional Interfaces* (Amsterdam: Elsevier, 2008).
10. See ibid., 86.
11. See again Dorau, *Emotionales Interaktionsdesign,* 178–79.
12. Jean-Luc Nancy, *Corpus* [1992], trans. Richard Rand (New York: Fordham University Press, 2000), 17.
13. See Luca Viglialoro, *Die Geste der Kunst: Paradigmen einer Ästhetik* (Bielefeld: transcript, 2021), 56.
14. Nancy, *Corpus,* 51.
15. See Matthias Bickenbach, “Knopfdruck und Auswahl: Zur taktilen Bildung technischer Medien”, *Zeitschrift für Literaturwissenschaft und Linguistik* 117 (2000): 9–32.
16. See ibid., 11.
17. See Marshall McLuhan, *Understanding Media: The Extensions of Man* [1964], (Cambridge: MIT Press, 1994); Vilém Flusser, Gestures [1974], trans. Nancy Ann Roth (Minneapolis: University of Minnesota Press, 2014).
18. See Oliver Ruf, “Wischen”, in *Historisches Wörterbuch des Mediengebrauchs,* ed. Heiko Christians, Matthias Bickenbach, and Nikolaus Wegmann (Cologne: Böhlau, 2015), 641–52.
19. See Susanne Knaller and Rita Rieger, ed., *Ästhetische Emotion: Formen und Figurationen zur Zeit des Umbruchs der Medien und Gattungen,* 1880–1959 (Heidelberg: Winter, 2016).
20. See Martina Ide, ed., *Ästhetik digitaler Medien: Aktuelle Perspektiven* (Bielefeld: transcript, 2022).
21. See Derrick de Kerckhove, “Touch versus Touch: Ästhetik neuer Technologien”, in *Die Aktualität des Ästhetischen,* ed. Wolfgang Welsch (München: Wilhelm Fink, 1993), 137–68, here 138.

Take Care – Thoughts on Tenderness in the Digital Age

Marie-France Rafael *takes care:* of the feeling she is hoping to find and the feelings that find her. In this excerpt, she paints pictures with our synapses – a chat between the nerve centre and the heart. A gentle knocking. Hello, are you there?

Marie-France Rafaelis is a professor at the Department of Art and Media at the Zurich University of the Arts in the theoretical field of contemporary art.

Gesture

She glanced down at her hands, which embraced her phone tightly. Instinctively, her thumb caressed the screen. She softly swiped her finger upward and then back down. In an abrupt move, she pressed the button on the right-hand side, and the screen went black. She tightened her fingers around the device even further, gripping it with both hands. She could feel it growing warmer and warmer in her grasp. The screen promptly lit up again. She must have brushed it accidentally. As if by chance, her fingertip traced the outline of her youngest child's still chubby face – the photo she'd always kept as her lock screen image.

A brush with tenderness

Still gazing at the picture of her child, a sight that always brought a smile to her lips, she wondered how many times a day she had held her two little ones in her arms, locked them in a tight embrace and tenderly caressed their faces. There must have been countless moments of closeness and affection. Once again, she became aware of the lukewarm metal in her hands and couldn't help but think that she interacted with and touched this technological device far more often than any human being around her. Could this be true? Something appeared on the screen again, interrupting her train of thought. Almost instinctively, she resumed her usual gestures: swiping, tapping, gliding her fingers along the gleaming glass surface at the end of her hand, which seemed on the verge of merging symbiotically with it.

Gestures

Her finger hung suspended in the air. Having just finished typing her response and hitting the send button, she attempted to resume her train of thought, although it proved somewhat elusive. She wondered about the kinds of gestures that consumed much of her day, as they had become more and more entwined with the operation, or should she say, the demands of her smartphone. Did she have control over these gestures, or were they controlling her – did the operation and aforementioned demands of her smartphone compel her to perform them? And she asked herself once again: what gestures were her hands performing?

In "Notes on Gesture", Giorgio Agamben characterises a gesture as a type of action in which "nothing is being produced or acted, but rather something is being endured and supported".[1] It exists, he says, in a realm of action that lies between *praxis* (action with the aim of producing a specific result) and *poiesis* (production that has "an end other than itself").[2] In this "in-between space", Agamben asserts, the *"gesture is the exhibition of a mediality: it is the process of making a means visible as such"*; it alludes to the "communication of a communicability".[3]

She felt certain that the gestures she made while interacting with her smartphone weren't just a means of operating the technical device but embodied the very essence of mediation itself. They had a self-reflexive quality, shaped by the interplay between operation, demand, and the question of control in the engagement with digital media. And yet the hands, in her view, added a further dimension to this understanding: amidst the destabilisation of lifestyles and the pervasive tendencies of alienation in our post-Fordist era – as highlighted by the Italian philosopher Paulo Virno, a prominent figure in the recent post-operaismo movement – that affect everyone equally, everyday gestures, expressed primarily through the hands, take on a new significance. She felt that in these times of changing living conditions as influenced by the digital age, and given the ubiquitous discussions about the role of humans vis-à-vis AI, insufficient attention was being paid to questions of gesture and the body, particularly the hands and especially in the context of digital technology use.

The French sociologist Michel de Certeau asserted that hands, originally created "for the plough, the typewriter, or the mill", cannot help but serve as a means of "linking people [...] to their surroundings".[4] Hands create, or could almost be called, a "site of tenderness". De Certeau goes on to say that hands carry "inherently within themselves an awareness of everyday things [...] so as to [recognise] nameless caresses or toils; and [have] the ability to convey what the intellect has not yet found words for, or perhaps has lost the ability to express".[5]

She thought about how the typewriter de Certeau mentions now finds its digital equivalent in the technologies we use to (and through which we) perform our everyday gestures – thanks in large part to our hands. Yet also she wondered whether these very technologies weren't increasingly keeping her from performing everyday tender gestures towards loved ones in the physical world. Was it not often the case – too often, in fact – that the sudden appearance of blue light on her smartphone screen immediately became the new focus of attention, thereby distancing her from those she holds most dear? Could it be that she felt closer and more connected to the photographs of her little ones that she was constantly clicking, scrolling, and sharing, than she did to the real people around her? She acknowledged her conflicting feelings. And she longed to change, or rather, to confront the alienating tendencies in her life with deeper introspection. Above all, she wanted to use her hands and gestures to discover a language of tenderness in day-to-day life – for herself and for her children, those she holds most dear.

1. Giorgio Agamben, "Notes on Gesture," in *Means Without End: Notes on Politics*, trans. Vincenzo Binetti and Cesare Casarino (Minneapolis: University of Minnesota Press, 2000), 48–60, here 57.
2. Ibid.
3. Ibid., 58 and 59.
4. Michel de Certeau, *GlaubensSchwachheit* (Stuttgart: Kohlhammer, 2009), 35.
5. Ibid.

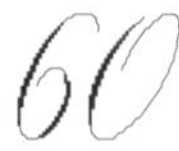

The Loneliness of the Female Astronaut

Oliver Bendel's selection from his collection of poems *Die Astronautin (The Female Astronaut)* looks at the loneliness experienced by a woman in space. The setting is an uninhabited location in which objects, plants, animals, and robots take on new meanings between longing and tenderness. At the same time, he invites readers to actively grapple with these poems, as if they were themselves traversing the cosmos, where nothing is simple or given. Doing so involves freeing the verses from their ornamental, coded trappings (they take the form of 3D codes with colour as the third dimension) and transforming them into readable, meaningful text with the aid of a JAB code reader (jabcode.org).

Oliver Bendel is a professor who researches and teaches information, robot and machine ethics at the School of Business FHNW. He has been a writer of experimental literature since 1984.

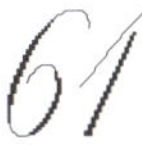

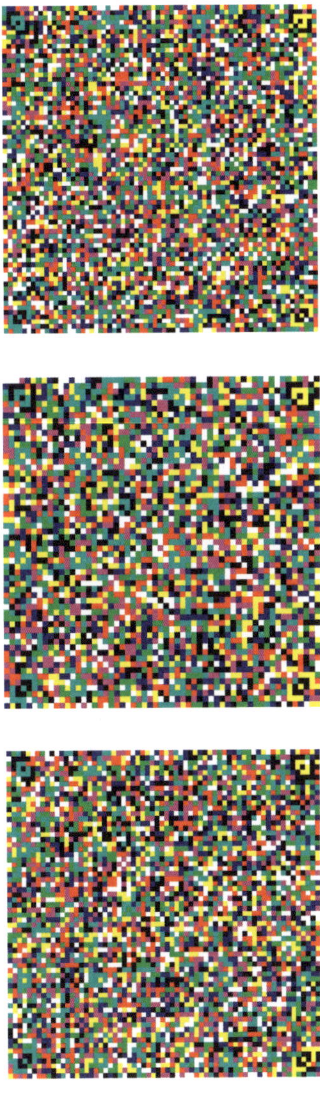

1 – Ein locker geflochtener Zopf
2 – Auf dem obersten Deck
3 – Seit Jahren spitzt sie den Bleistift

Transitions and Thresholds

Spoiler alert: life will kill us in the end. Data meets its demise differently from humans, and loved ones can grieve and *death chat* with the deceased via data. Sociologist Francis Müller explores these issues in a look at the interplay between digitality, life, death and dying.

Francis Müller is a lecturer and researcher in the Trends & Identity department at Zurich University of the Arts.

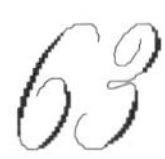

Dying confronts us with existential contradictions: the absolute certainty that we will die is juxtaposed with the equally absolute uncertainty of what death, after the process of dying, actually entails. From a medical point of view, dying is characterised by the cessation of organ functions leading to the death of a living being. However, dying also encompasses social, cultural, religious, and philosophical dimensions that vary historically. In Europe, for example, religious institutions long had a monopoly on the transition to the afterlife, adorning it with symbols and rituals. With the advent of secularisation, institutionalised religion was de-institutionalised and privatised, relinquishing its monopoly over these final transitions. However, religion did not disappear;[1] it underwent a transformation[2] – and found its place in the digital realm as well. Thanks to positivism and the rise of individualism, there has been a shift in emphasis "away from death as such and towards the process of dying".[3]

This shift in focus is further accentuated by socio-demographic trends: according to the Swiss Federal Statistical Office (FSO), life expectancy in Switzerland has doubled over the past 150 years thanks to medical advances.[4] This trend is not limited to Western countries, but is largely global.[5] Worldwide, people live longer, but they are also increasingly susceptible to age-related diseases. Because modern medicine can manage many of these diseases, we live longer with serious conditions. As a result, people spend more time in the dying phase, which begins with the diagnosis of terminal illness and ends with death. In these dying stages, the traditional medical ethos of preserving life becomes less relevant, while palliative care, which is primarily concerned with minimising suffering, is given greater precedence. Terminally ill people often find themselves in so-called *settings of dying*[6], which is to say institutional contexts such as palliative care units, hospices or home-based palliative care. In these settings, life worlds are transformed into "death worlds"[7], where the process of dying is both "done"[8] and "designed"[9].

Settings of dying are characterised by their spatial, material, and social "smallness". Typically, the physical space is limited to a single room with a bed. Social interactions are limited to close family members, health professionals, and pastoral care. The number of objects present in these settings is reduced, with items such as personal care products, medical equipment, personal belongings (books, mementos, photographs), and sometimes religiously symbolic items (Buddha figures, crosses, angels, crystals, stones) being common. In addition, technological objects such as smartphones and tablets are increasingly found in these settings. Settings of dying are on the one hand located in the realm of the living, yet they also serve as gateways to other transcendent worlds. They function as transitional spaces, marking the passage between the earthly and the hereafter.

Digital technologies also facilitate a transcendence of the limited here and now. To begin with, digital media such as smartphones or tablets have a tangible materiality. In physical terms, they represent intimate "possession markers" that as "personal effects, [constitute] a preserve in their own right, are frequently employed as markers; moving them or even touching them is something like touching their owner's body"[10]. Drawing on her research into young people and their smartphones, Heather Horst refers to "mobile intimacies"[11]. The reluctance to lend smartphones[12] can also be attributed to the personal data stored on the devices or in the cloud. This data serves as an "information preserve"[13], containing personal and intimate details about individuals. Consequently, it is crucial for people in end-of-life situations to have their smartphones close at hand. Designer Bitten Stetter, who researches and designs in the field of palliative care,[14] was inspired to create a "bed box" for this purpose. The boxes allow people in settings of dying to keep important and personal items close to their bodies.[15]

The terminally ill can engage in new forms of social interaction through digital practices. Cultural scientist Gaudenz Metzger interviewed a dying man[16] who took photographs of birds outside his hospice window and shared them on Facebook, where they received likes and comments.[17] This act of photo-sharing led to social interactions and more fluid forms of social engagement. In addition, tools such as Google Street View allow people facing terminal illness to travel virtually to distant locations, allowing them to revisit cherished cities or explore places they have long wanted to visit but never had the chance to. They can converse with people who are far away, experiencing the other person's voice, body language, and facial expressions through visual and auditory means. In this way, absent individuals become accessible within one's own subjective space. Even aspects of intimacy, eroticism, and tenderness can be experienced digitally and sometimes even physically.[18]

In the moments before death, individuals are confronted with existential questions that go beyond the realm of answers provided by reductionist sciences. As a result, spiritual experiences and religious interpretations often take on greater significance in these circumstances. Questions of dying, death, religion, and the afterlife are also being discussed in the digital sphere: Cowan and Hadden use the term "online religion"[19] to describe emerging forms of religious communication in the digital domain.[20] This term encompasses digital interactions that explore the double valuation of the immanent and the transcendent;[21] concepts such as "soul", "God", "angels", and "nirvana" allude to transcendence, pointing to dimensions beyond our immediate world. These terms serve as attempts to frame the transcendent, and even personal experiences of transcendence, through symbols and concepts.[22] It is worth noting that accounts of internal struggles with "doubts in faith" are another form of religious communication.[23] A plethora of death blogs on the Internet bear witness to these profound journeys of faith exploration.[24]

After death, digital interactions continue. Firstly, there are numerous forums where the bereaved process their grief,[25] recognising that death, as Norbert Elias articulated, is not a problem for the deceased, but for the living.[26] Many people continue to exist digitally in a state of "memorial mode"; they remain present on Facebook, in digital cemeteries or, through the use of artificial intelligence, even manifest themselves as chatbots.[27] These chatbots, sometimes referred to as "deathbots", have internalised the linguistic patterns of specific individuals and can engage in communicative exchanges, facilitating conversations and even "encounters" with the deceased. In South Korea, for example, a mother used virtual reality technology to meet her three-year-old daughter, who had previously died of an illness. This extraordinary event was documented on film,[28] showing the mother wearing VR goggles and trying to touch her daughter, who was visible in the virtual world. The mother's emotional reaction after the encounter was evident. This demonstrates that digitality is not just "cold", but has the capacity to evoke intense emotions and create states of suspension and transition – elements that are also integral to farewell rituals and rites of passage.[29] Another noteworthy instance involves the Mexican journalist Javier Valdez. Following his murder in 2017 in the state of Sinaloa as a result of his investigative efforts on the Mexican drug war, a digital representation resembling him emerged three years later. This digital avatar garnered considerable attention by shedding light on social disparities and the alarming levels of violence in Mexico. It also took on a unique role as a posthumous advocate in the digital sphere, directing its messages towards President Andrés Manuel López Obrador.[30]

These examples illustrate that digitalisation is not only infiltrating our daily lives, but also our dying. It does so quietly and subtly, but its impact is all the more profound. Digitalisation gains importance in the pre-mortal stages of life, where it "accompanies" us through transitions. These digital remnants, data, information, and virtual identities remain in the world after our death, raising ethical and legal questions, such as who actually owns this data. The deceased may "rest" in a digital cemetery, or they may be "brought back to life" and into the world. Cultural fabrics have been woven through these digital realms, entangling us in pre- and post-mortem spheres.

1. Peter L. Berger, ed., *The Desecularization of the World: Resurgent Religion and World Politics* (Michigan: William B. Eerdmans, 1999).
2. Thomas Luckmann, *The Invisible Religion: The Problem of Religion in Modern Society* (New York: Macmillan, 1967).
3. Petra Gehring, *Theorien des Todes zur Einführung* (Hamburg: Junius, 2010), 167.

4. Swiss Federal Statistical Office, ed., *Demografisches Porträt der Schweiz. Bestand, Struktur und Bevölkerung im Jahr 2020* (Neuchâtel: Bundesamt für Statistik, 2022), 21.
5. People in sub-Saharan Africa have also lived much longer in recent decades than in the past. See United Nations, Department of Economic and Social Affairs, Population Division, *World Mortality 2019: Highlights* (= ST/ESA/SER.A/432, New York: United Nations, 2019), 6–7.
6. The Swiss National Science Foundation (SNF) project of the same name, titled "Settings of Dying: An Interdisciplinary Perspective 2020–2023" is based on a joint project of the Bern University of Applied Sciences (BFH) and the Zurich University of the Arts (ZHdK). See "Settings of Dying", Sterbesettings, accessed September 5, 2023, sterbesettings.ch/en
7. Martin W. Schnell, Werner Schneider, and Harald J. Kolbe, *Sterbewelten. Eine Ethnographie* (Wiesbaden: Springer, 2014).
8. Werner Schneider, "Sterbewelten: Ethnographische (und dispositivanalytische) Forschung zum Lebensende," in Schnell, Schneider, and Kolbe, *Sterbewelten,* 51–138, here 62.
9. Corina Caduff et al., *Sterben Gestalten* (Zurich: Scheidegger & Spiess, forthcoming).
10. Erving Goffman, *Relations in Public: Microstudies of the Public Order* (New York: Basic Books, 1971), 42.
11. Heather Horst, "Mobile Intimicies: Everyday Design and the Aesthetics of Mobile Phones", in *Digital Materialities: Design and Anthropology,* ed. Sarah Pink, Elisenda Ardèvol and Débora Lanzeni (London: Bloomsbury, 2016), 159–74.
12. Bernt Schnettler, "Digitale Alltagsfotografie und visuelles Wissen", in *Fotografie und Gesellschaft: Phänomenologische und wissenssoziologische Perspektiven,* ed. Thomas S. Eberle (Bielefeld: transcript, 2017), 242–55, here 246.
13. Goffman, *Relations in Public,* 39.
14. Among other things, in the context of the SNF project "Settings of Dying", see n6.
15. Bitten Stetter and Francis Müller, "Dinge am Lebensende: Eine designethnografische Studie", in *Lebenswelten gestalten: Neue Felder & Forschungszugänge einer Designanthropologie,* ed. Michaela Fenske and Isabella Kölz (Würzburg: Königshausen & Neumann, 2022), 183–207, here 194–95.
16. In the context of the SNF project "Settings of Dying", see n6.
17. Gaudenz U. Metzger, "Draußen, die Vögel: Foto-Sharing im letzten Lebensabschnitt einer chronisch kranken Person", in *Jahrbuch für Tod und Gesellschaft 2023,* ed. Thorsten Benkel and Matthias Meitzler (Weinheim: Beltz Juventa, 2023), 69–89, here 82–84.
18. An example of the experience of digital tenderness and eroticism is the phenomenon of Autonomous Sensory Meridian Response (ASMR). This refers to a tingling and soothing sensation that can be generated through gentle touching on the head, as well as specific sounds like whispering or lip sounds. See Jade Wu Savy, "Is ASMR Real or Just a Pseudoscience?", Scientific American, December 4, 2019, www.scientificamerican.com/article/is-asmr-real-or-just-a-pseudoscience
    Acoustic stimuli can be experienced purely digitally and can indeed evoke physiological responses. The degree of eroticism can vary greatly. See Mark Hay, "ASMR Is Supposedly Nonsexual. So Why Is There So Much ASMR Porn?" *Mashable,* May 4, 2022, mashable.com/article/asmr-porn-fusion
19. Douglas E. Cowan and Jeffrey K. Hadden, "Virtually Religious: The New Religious Movements and the World Wide Web", in *The Oxford Handbook of New Religious Movements,* ed. James R. Lewis (New York: University Press, 2004), 119–40, here 120.
20. This contrasts with "religion online", which describes the digital presence of religious organisations (e.g., the website of a church congregation, a mosque, a Buddhist temple, etc.).
21. Niklas Luhmann, *A Systems Theory of Religion,* ed. André Kieserling, trans. David A. Brenner with Adrian Hermann (Stanford: Stanford University Press, 2013), 77.
22. Francis Müller and Gaudenz Metzger, "Transzendente Erfahrungen rahmen", in *Kontext Sterben,* ed. Corina Caduff et al. (Zurich: Scheidegger & Spiess, 2022), 156–65.
23. Niklas Luhmann, *A Systems Theory of Religion,* 166.
24. Corina Caduff, "Veröffentlichte Sterbeerfahrung", in *Kontext Sterben,* ed. Corina Caduff et al. (Zurich: Scheidegger & Spiess, 2022), 32–48, here 33–38.
25. Beaunoyera et al., "Grieving in the Digital Era: Mapping Online Support for Grief and Bereavement", *Patient Education and Counseling* 103, no. 12 (2020): 215–24.
26. Norbert Elias, *The Loneliness of the Dying,* trans. Edmund Jephcott (New York/London: Continuum, 2001), 3.
27. Steve Przybilla, "Chatten mit Toten: Wie Chatbots den ewigen Dialog ermöglichen", *Neue Zürcher Zeitung,* July 10, 2021, www.nzz.ch/gesellschaft/kuenstliche-intelligenz-dank-chatbot-im-dialog-mit-toten-bleiben-ld.1632459
28. Global News, "Virtual Reality 'Reunites' Mother with Dead Daughter in South Korean Doc", YouTube video, February 14, 2020, youtu.be/0p8HZVCZSkc?feature=shared
29. Victor Turner, *The Ritual Process: Structure and Anti-Structure* (Ithaca, New York: Cornell University Press, 2005).
30. Propuestacivicamx, "Javier Valdez habla a 3 años de su asesinato #SeguimosHablando", YouTube video, October 29, 2020, youtu.be/h1PbP-whfrY?feature=shared

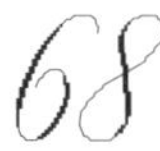

The Night Remains

In this autofictional writing project, Leoni Hof reflects on the consequences of a father's death and the efforts to preserve his memory. The narrator describes her search for him online, especially through the use of ChatGPT, an artificial intelligence. She hopes to find some hint of him in the digital realm. This essay explores the fleeting nature of memories and how we can recover them in virtual worlds. Or not.

Leoni Hof is Journalist, Author and co-leads the Content and PR team at ZHdK University Communications.

My father died in August. I decided not to remember the exact day. Right from the start, I forbade myself to recall it. I forced myself to forget the date. I had no desire to be reminded of it. Didn't want to startle every year on that day. Shocked, as if I would always forget what had happened all over again. I've had trouble recalling numbers ever since. Birthdays elude me, as do mobile numbers. I do not know my salary or my bank balance. The numbers slip from my mind like Mikado sticks on a table. Repulsed, I try to grasp them with trembling fingers. And accidentally scatter the whole pile.

I sometimes search for him at night. Type his name into the Google search bar. I ask ChatGPT, what do you know about this man? And the machine won't even make something up. Clear, ruthless, relentless. "I'm sorry, but I cannot find any information on this person." My father died in August. Just before we all plunged into the WWW and the world expanded so much after those shrill modem beeps. Out, out, out of here was all I wanted. And a small bum. On that first day of the rest of my life, I contemplated my posterior. I wondered if it would look fat in the trousers I had borrowed from my mother. I had nothing black in my wardrobe for the funeral. I would spend the rest of my life as a half-orphan. I rolled the word around in my mouth, whispered it secretly in the bathroom. Pronounced it to myself as if I were learning a new word. I was many things. Almost of age, soon to be an A-level student. I'd never been a half-orphan before. I didn't know how to fill that word in. What it meant to be a half-orphan, inside and out. How to speak, look and bear it. If you could choose it. If you had a choice.

I remember the mist that suddenly enveloped everything. It came from Dad's pills. Dad was always on edge, a force to be reckoned with. Tall and broad, and when he wasn't cheerful, he was sad. He had hidden the tablets among socks and fabric handkerchiefs. Some of them had monograms. Sometimes, all that remains of a person is their initials on a handkerchief. There was nothing else to remember him by. No books with notes scribbled in the margins, no collection of travel souvenirs or quirky bric-a-brac. Something that hinted at its owner. How is it possible for someone to leave so little behind? He left us two notes. Square ones, torn from the kitchen notepad. You could still see the indented lines of his farewell as we later wrote our shopping lists. On the day my father died, I took one of his worn T-shirts from the laundry. I followed his scent trail. Eventually, there was nothing left of him in it. There was just me and CK One.

Had I known the answer, my father would still be alive. “What should I do?” he had asked. As he gathered my hair at the nape of my neck, just as he had done when I was a child. I wasn’t entirely sure I liked it. I kept quiet. Our physical contact at that time was limited to random bumps and jostles. This gathering of my hair must have taken me aback. “Just don’t go on like this,” I had said. He had taken me at my word. And didn’t go on.

When I search for my father at night, I lie down under the living room table. I lie there and I google his name. I type in the area where he lived, his job. I can’t think of much else about him. Not much to feed the search engine. I imagine I’ll find him if I just remember more. Come on, ChatGPT, just make something up! Zeros and ones for all I care, a virtual echo from the other side. “As an AI language model, I am programmed not to give false or misleading information.” AI is an asshole. My father died in August.

“ […]
I ask ChatGPT,
what do you know
about this man?
↘
And the machine
won’t even
make
something
up.
⁑

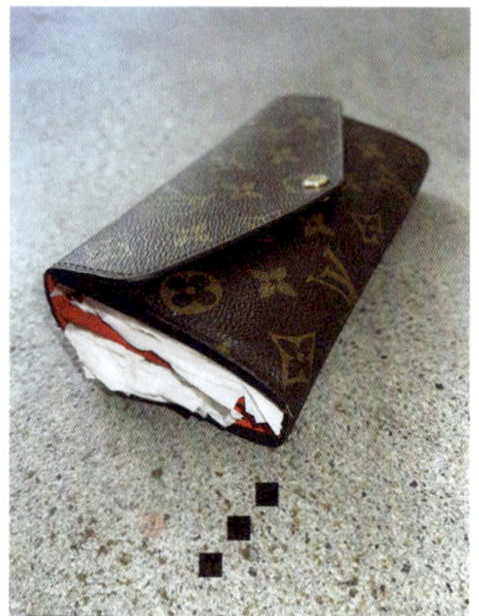

Empty and Space

The age of digital connectivity finds us striving to connect places that had not been connected before. The result is an ever-denser network of lines. And yet what is left untouched, unaffected by all this? Dead angles, blind spots, black holes, realms of non-being, open spaces offering us the luxury of expansion, of deconvolution. Marisa Burn paints a light-net of silence, of tender nothingness, with luminance and line.

Marisa Burn is co-founder of House of Change, leads the CAS Digital Learning and Teaching Cultures and programme manager of the educational formats for E-Learning, Learning & Teaching Dossier of the Zurich University of the Arts.

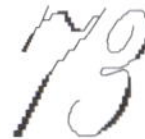

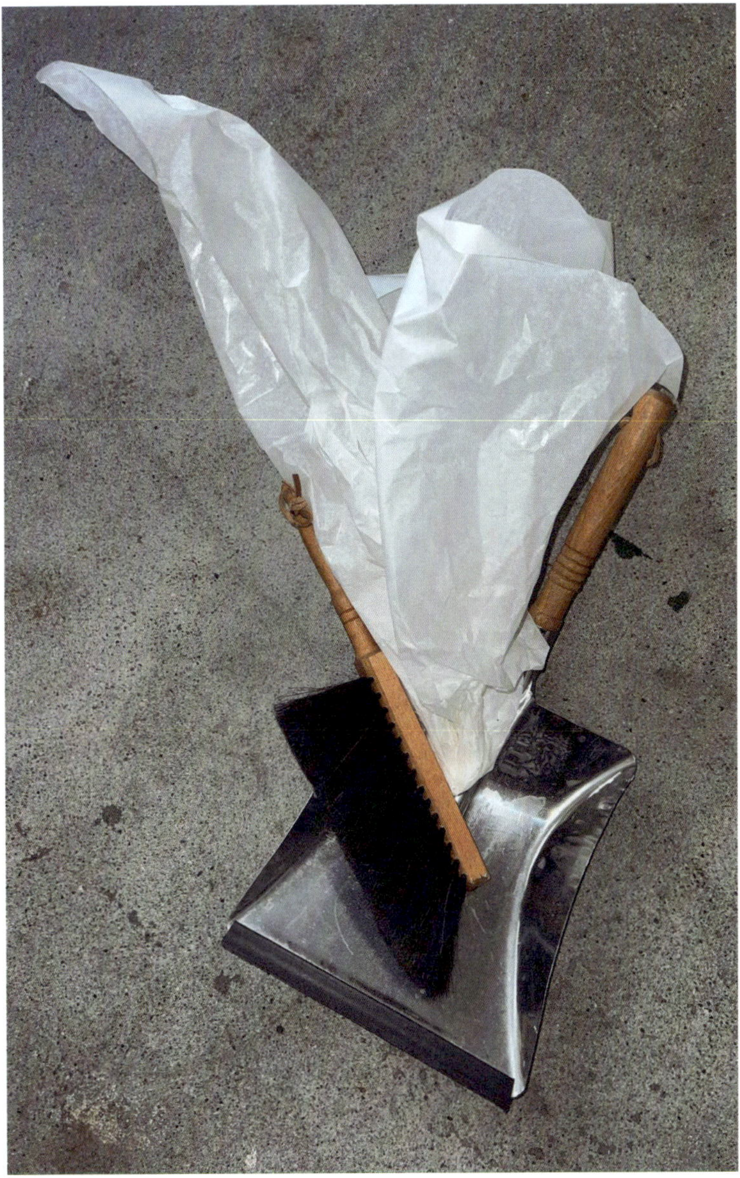

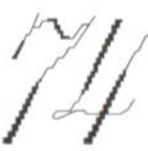

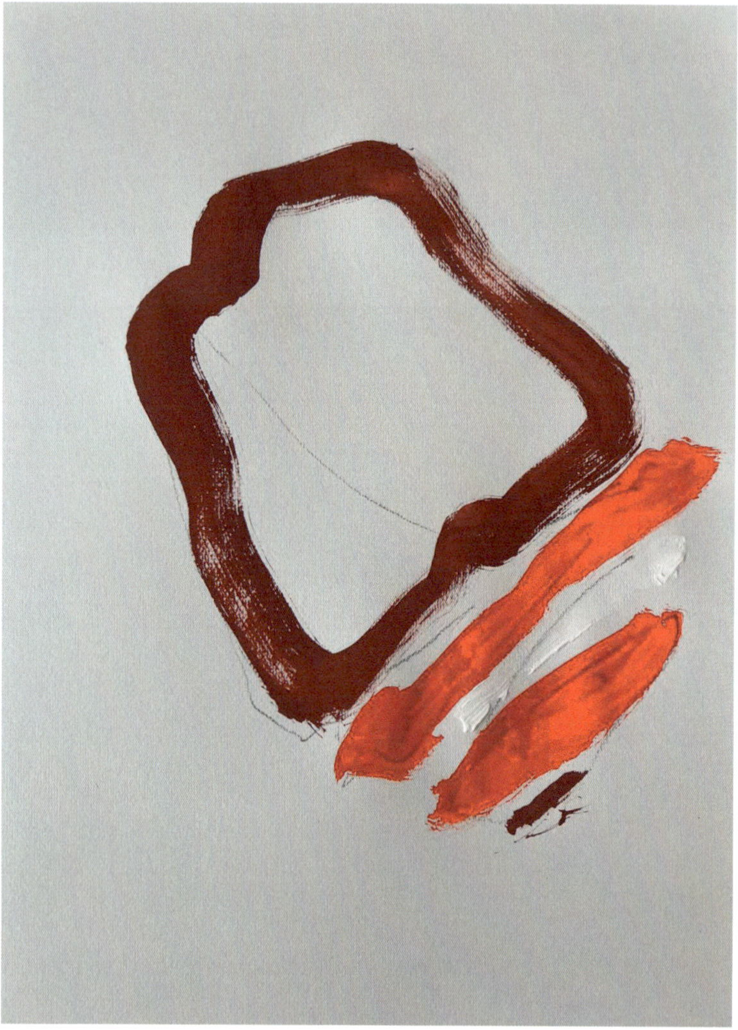

Marisa Burn

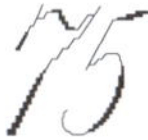

Empty and Space

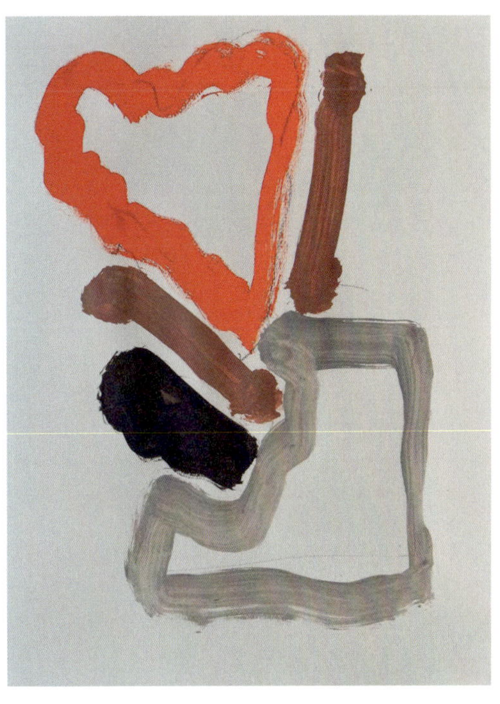

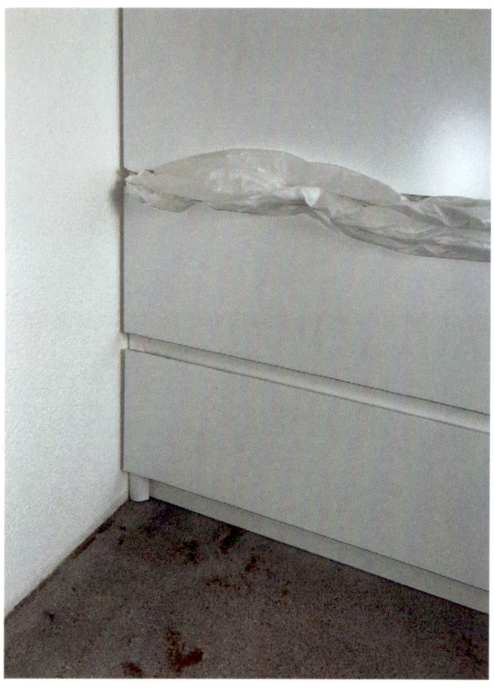

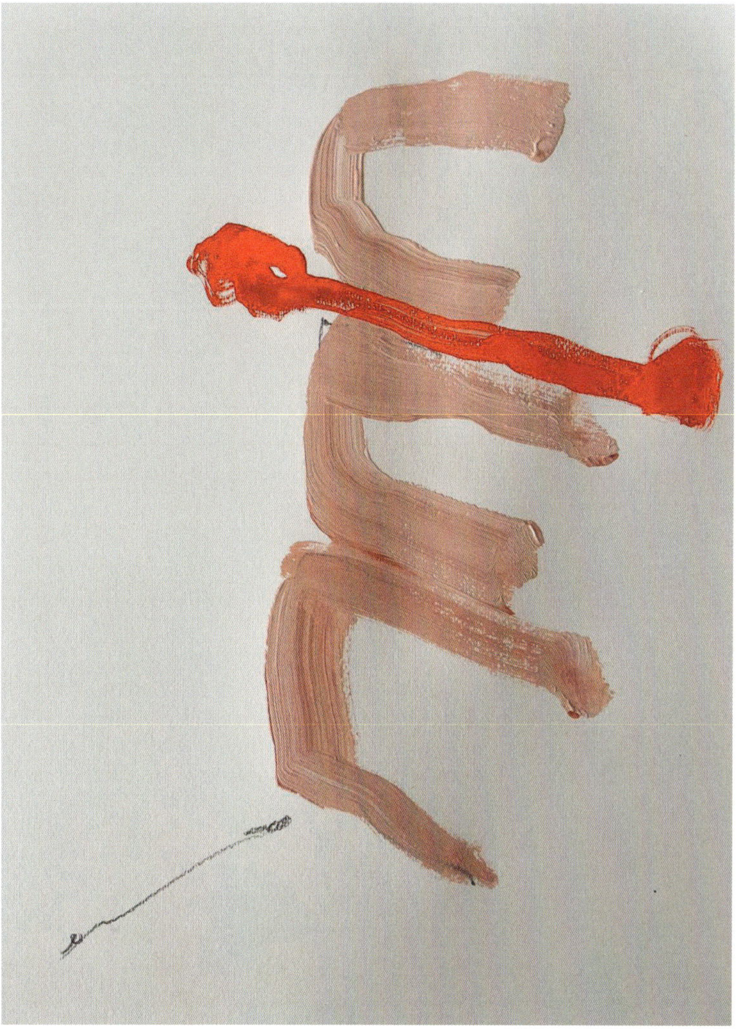

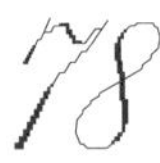

The New Research Program

The New Research Program: nor blow nor kiss but tender understanding and emphatic transformation – Alexander Damianisch's poetic words are not as tender as they seem. His perspective reveals a powerful and radical understanding of what it means to be an activist. What it means to be tender, strong, and politically active. His mission is to make creative, cultural, and artistic practice as acceptable as other disciplines. What's more: maybe, just maybe, his mission is not only his. It should be a transnational one – our mission! Because art is the future, art is now.

Alexander Damianisch heads the Center Research Focus and is responsible for project development in art and research at the University of Applied Arts Vienna.

The gap, the practice
Between the instrument and the mission, I have to say in advance that when I think about research in the arts and sciences, I am increasingly concerned with the question of this gap, the gap that politics leave, or, in other words: how to describe what is lost in the moment of transition. Because the terms, instruments and mission that are currently being centrally negotiated span a horizon that ignores the heart of the matter. Here we have concepts such as mission-oriented research; there we have, for example, digitality, Janus-faced as an utopian or dystopian offer of an ideal or simply lost future. The strategies are determined by the perception of the mission, its definition and mandate, and the action on the instrument, its design and development. But what is crucial is openness, and how to accept what is really important, the practice of it.

The transition, the flight
The in-between, for me, is the moment of transition. It is about the flight, not the hand that throws, or the hand that catches. My impression is that the sensitive handling of the possibilities of flight is not given enough attention when it comes to securing conditions. The mission and the instrument are very important, this should by no means be disputed, but it is essential not to leave the definition to these two factors. The path must follow the practice of scientific or artistic research and the diversity of artistic and scientific methods within it. Especially when it is essential, when the path is not a straight line, because it is only in deviation that change in our understanding takes place. When I think about research in art and science, I think about having to discover new things with an open mind.

Resistant, tender
The issue of digitalisation permeates all areas of social context. This penetration is impressive in its benefits and power. Personally and institutionally, we are increasingly supported digitally and determined, both thematically and methodologically. The digital as an instrument is increasingly shaping our current presence in all areas. I advocate a certain resistance, but I would like to call it sensitivity, thereby using the concept of digital tenderness, simply following

the old motto that where there is danger, the good grows too. The digital is an essential form of media that we can and must use. However, it must not be designed in a deterministic and functionalistic way, because then it will not achieve its potential but only fulfil expectations.

Understanding and transforming

A programme of flight must create margins that are as open as possible and only as narrow as necessary. Gaps are not easy to close, they have to be exploited. I am convinced that this must be a programme of transformation of understanding and understanding of transformation; a programme that continually wants to understand itself anew and that, in addition to its conditionality, also tries to take a curious look at everything that is and can be or could be. This would be the ideal programme of new research, and the separation between the throwing hand, the flight and the target would no longer be possible, because everything would be tenderly brought into the open moment of prudence, of constant confrontation and ongoing reconfiguration.

Quality of tenderness

What qualities should the transformation programme have? The focus is on the gap between mission and instrument; I wish this programme would be one in which quality of tenderness is taken seriously. Here I am taking up the term offered and trying to make it usable. I see tenderness as a quality of orientation that brings new relevance to serious play. Tenderness is a value of affective closeness that seeks closeness and respect for subject and object. Tenderness is a value of open circumspection, prudent openness, respect and empathy. If this tenderness succeeds, then I can imagine a digitality that, as an instrument, finds fewer weaponised mouths than mouths of resonance, and more open than closed missions.

Deflection of the circles

The mission and the digital are two guiding concepts for art and science, for teaching and research discourse, which threaten to obscure other potentials. It is essential not to forget these. This

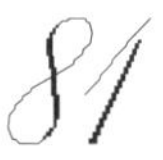

preoccupation runs the risk of distracting us from what really needs to be done: shaping the space in-between, taking care of what has to happen immediately, in concrete form. How can we transform understanding and understand transformation, using all the methods of insight-oriented practice, so that serendipity does not always have to be used as a creative excuse for a "the-exception-proves-the-rule approach"? It also seems to me that these aspects of mission and instrument give the impression that the essential cycle has been recognised, when at best you are creating a cycle that does not run smoothly, but rather just bumps along, at the two points that are probably not quite the most essential, but not at rest, either.

Supply and demand

The mission can be understood as a goal developed through strategy, born of a certain interest orientation, whereby the word "mission", unlike "interest", also contains an overarching moral rightness, which makes the word seem particularly righteous. This meaning is in fact precisely what should not be the focus in the context of insight-oriented and understanding practice, because it is not free of answers, as one could polemically say to those who have them. The term "instrument", on the other hand, refers to that used to pursue interests, whereby the instrument, unlike the tool, has a meaning that also extends to the sensory experience of its development. This makes the instrument likeable. There is, however, a danger that the instrument, handled with virtuosity, will become a trap that, when mastered with excellence, no longer contains any tenderness, which means that it is no longer a game.

Today, the mission is determined, on the one hand, by the ever-clamouring borders and their increasing power of definition and, on the other, by the consequent need to address the barriers and expand the circles of influence again. The inner mission is determined by an intense presence of precariousness. Instruments are understood as promises to solve problems. It is not uncommon, however, for their supply to outstrip demand.

Tender comrade

"Tender Comrade" is the name of a song that asks what happens to those who have returned from a mission – I'll leave it open in which context – and now find themselves back in the world whose rules were thrown out of order while deployed. What do you do when the mission is over? What happens to the instruments? How long or short is the half-life of instruments when the job is done?

What do we do with the digitality that we brought into the world and now want to make disappear because it was only a step, not a path itself, or a dance. Here too, the promise is that we will create tools that will help us better overcome challenges, also as epistemic objects.

Claim and reality

It would be nice if we could apply the concept of tenderness when it comes to using what is available to us in a different way, that is, tenderly, carefully and cautiously, trying to understand each other not as intruders but as partners. The digital is one instrument among many that we can use, not as an end in itself, but as one among many that can help us transform our understanding and understand this transformation. There are many missions that shouldn't change, and once again we are able to expand our circles of influence, with the aim of transforming our understanding and gaining a new understanding of this transformation in the real world.

Throw and flight

When moving, the direction must be changed carefully. If other forms promise more than one assumed, then a throw becomes a flight. Thanks to tender digitality, a blow becomes a kiss. So what is there to be done? Let's take up the politics of enabling.

" [...]
The inner mission
is determined
↘
by an intense
presence
of
precariousness.
⁑

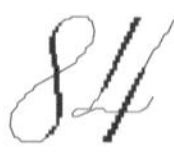

Traces of a Lost Relationship

Erasure, absence and illusion. Léa Ermuth reflects on the sudden resurfacing of bygones. Can history be reimagined, or how can stories be saved from oblivion? Is it the connections themselves that fade – the ties that bind us? A ‹Can you hear me?› echoes through the ether. Some connections find their place in the archives, others mark the start of something new.

Léa Ermuth is a communications manager at Zurich University of the Arts and a designer whose practice blends digital and analogue fabrication methods.

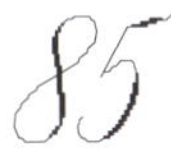

Traces of a Lost Relationship

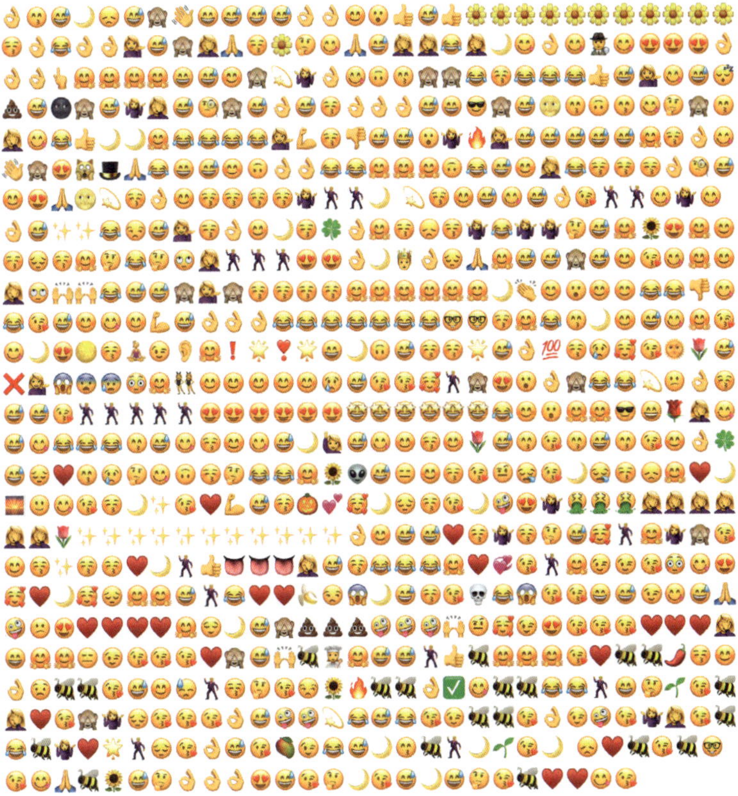

Delete. I don't know exactly when I did it, but I did it – I deleted the chat history between my ex and me. More than three years later, I feel the urge to revisit the digital traces of our one-year long-distance relationship. Fortunately, I can rely on my ex in this situation and so I received our digital archive of past messages as an export folder. It now resides on my laptop in the form of a .txt file. I appreciate the simplicity of its presentation; it has a certain raw, neutral quality. I'm still saved as "Lea the endangered species", a moniker coined at our first meeting when a stranger remarked that my red-orange hair was "on the verge of dying out".

By the time I returned to my former home in Amsterdam, screens had become a crux of our relationships and pixels had replaced physical touch. Technology can cultivate an intimacy that defies geographical distance. But in what way? "We slip into thinking that always being connected is going to make us less lonely. But we are at risk because it is actually the reverse," writes psychologist Sherry Turkle in her book Reclaiming Conversation (2015). As I sift through the endless messages, a sense of melancholy washes over me, and I'm reminded that connectivity really doesn't automatically banish loneliness. I think what Turkle is saying is that technology falls into a paradox – it connects us, but the inability to be physically present leaves us longing. Or, as Turkle put it, "If we are unable to be alone, we will be more lonely".

Missed phone calls are becoming a silent means of escaping feelings of isolation. Technology allows us to be ever-present in each other's lives, instantly and continuously in touch. But what are the implications? How deep does this digitality go? How tender is it really? I notice an abundance of emojis. These little pictorial expressions have likewise become part of our language. Amid the constant barrage of notifications and pings, the line between disconnection and connection is blurring. "In the new communication culture, interruption is not experienced as interruption but as another connection," Turkle observes. In her 2014 book Addiction by Design: Machine Gambling in Las Vegas, anthropologist Natasha Dow Schüll introduced the term "machine zone" to describe a state of mind in which the line between self and technology becomes blurred. In a perpetual machine zone state, technological communication feels

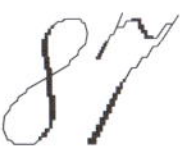

Traces of a Lost Relationship

👌👌👌👌👌👌👌👌👌👌👌👌👌👌👌👌👌👌👌👌👌👌👌👌👌👌👌👌👌👌
👌👌👌👌👌👌👌👌👌👌👌👌
😙😙😙😙😙😙😙😙😙😙😙😙
😅😅😅😅😅😅😅😅😅😅😅😅😅😅😅😅😅😅😅😅😅😅😅😅😅😅😅😅😅😅
😅😅😅😅😅😅😅😅😅😅😅😅😅😅😅😅😅😅😅😅😅😅😅😅😅😅😅😅😅😅
😅😅😅😅😅😅😅😅😅😅😅😅😅😅😅😅😅
🌙🌙🌙🌙🌙🌙🌙🌙🌙🌙🌙🌙🌙🌙🌙🌙🌙🌙🌙🌙🌙🌙🌙🌙🌙🌙
😞😞😞😞
🙈🙈🙈🙈🙈🙈🙈🙈🙈🙈🙈🙈🙈🙈🙈🙈🙈🙈🙈
👋👋
😁😁😁😁😁😁😁😁😁
😊😊😊😊😊😊😊😊😊😊😊😊😊😊😊😊😊😊😊😊😊😊😊😊😊😊😊😊😊😊
😊😊
😮😮😮😮😮
👍👍👍👍👍
🌼🌼🌼🌼🌼🌼🌼🌼🌼🌼🌼🌼
😚😚😚😚😚😚😚😚😚😚😚😚😚😚😚😚😚😚😚😚😚😚😚😚😚😚😚😚😚😚
😚😚😚😚😚😚😚😚😚😚😚😚😚😚😚😚😚😚😚
😂😂😂😂😂😂😂😂😂😂😂😂😂😂😂😂😂😂😂😂😂😂😂😂😂😂😂😂😂😂
😂😂😂😂😂😂😂😂😂😂😂😂😂😂😂😂😂😂😂😂
💁‍♀️💁‍♀️💁‍♀️💁‍♀️💁‍♀️💁‍♀️💁‍♀️
🤦‍♀️
🤷‍♀️🤷‍♀️🤷‍♀️🤷‍♀️🤷‍♀️🤷‍♀️🤷‍♀️🤷‍♀️🤷‍♀️🤷‍♀️🤷‍♀️🤷‍♀️🤷‍♀️🤷‍♀️
🕵️‍♂️
🙏🙏🙏🙏🙏🙏🙏
🤔🤔🤔🤔🤔🤔🤔🤔🤔🤔🤔🤔🤔
😋😋😋😋😋😋😋😋😋😋😋😋😋😋😋😋😋😋😋😋😋😋😋😋😋😋😋😋😋
😍😍😍😍😍😍😍😍😍😍😍😍😍😍😍😍😍😍😍😍😍
👆
🤗🤗🤗🤗🤗🤗🤗🤗🤗🤗🤗🤗🤗🤗🤗🤗🤗🤗🤗🤗🤗🤗🤗🤗🤗🤗🤗🤗🤗🤗
🤗🤗🤗🤗🤗🤗🤗🤗🤗🤗
💫💫💫💫💫
🙃🙃🙃🙃🙃🙃
😴
💩💩💩💩
🌚
🧐🧐
😎😎
🌝🌝

[21.09.18, 17:43:07] lea die aussterbende spezies: Verpasster Sprachanruf
[29.09.18, 19:18:34] lea die aussterbende spezies: Verpasster Sprachanruf
[03.10.18, 14:49:02] lea die aussterbende spezies: Verpasster Sprachanruf
[03.10.18, 14:57:34] lea die aussterbende spezies: Verpasster Sprachanruf
[03.10.18, 17:46:09] lea die aussterbende spezies: Verpasster Sprachanruf
[03.10.18, 22:13:30] lea die aussterbende spezies: Verpasster Sprachanruf
[04.10.18, 16:00:55] lea die aussterbende spezies: Verpasster Sprachanruf
[10.10.18, 17:58:51] lea die aussterbende spezies: Verpasster Sprachanruf
[11.10.18, 21:20:26] lea die aussterbende spezies: Verpasster Sprachanruf
[15.10.18, 21:40:41] lea die aussterbende spezies: Verpasster Sprachanruf
[22.10.18, 22:29:09] lea die aussterbende spezies: Verpasster Sprachanruf
[23.10.18, 18:43:24] lea die aussterbende spezies: Verpasster Sprachanruf
[26.10.18, 20:00:48] lea die aussterbende spezies: Verpasster Sprachanruf
[26.10.18, 21:36:06] lea die aussterbende spezies: Verpasster Sprachanruf
[27.10.18, 19:50:08] lea die aussterbende spezies: Verpasster Sprachanruf
[28.10.18, 15:36:25] lea die aussterbende spezies: Verpasster Sprachanruf
[04.11.18, 22:45:33] lea die aussterbende spezies: Verpasster Sprachanruf
[08.11.18, 23:01:16] lea die aussterbende spezies: Verpasster Sprachanruf
[15.11.18, 19:50:40] lea die aussterbende spezies: Verpasster Sprachanruf
[15.11.18, 20:40:36] lea die aussterbende spezies: Verpasster Sprachanruf
[19.11.18, 16:21:09] lea die aussterbende spezies: Verpasster Sprachanruf
[19.11.18, 16:21:27] lea die aussterbende spezies: Verpasster Sprachanruf
[22.11.18, 19:51:41] lea die aussterbende spezies: Verpasster Sprachanruf
[23.11.18, 16:57:08] lea die aussterbende spezies: Verpasster Sprachanruf
[27.11.18, 23:30:04] lea die aussterbende spezies: Verpasster Sprachanruf
[27.11.18, 23:30:02] lea die aussterbende spezies: Verpasster Sprachanruf
[02.12.18, 22:16:40] lea die aussterbende spezies: Verpasster Sprachanruf
[04.12.18, 23:16:25] lea die aussterbende spezies: Verpasster Sprachanruf
[04.12.18, 23:16:40] lea die aussterbende spezies: Verpasster Sprachanruf
[07.12.18, 00:04:11] lea die aussterbende spezies: Verpasster Sprachanruf
[07.12.18, 00:04:36] lea die aussterbende spezies: Verpasster Sprachanruf
[08.12.18, 21:15:22] lea die aussterbende spezies: Verpasster Sprachanruf
[09.12.18, 23:01:38] lea die aussterbende spezies: Verpasster Sprachanruf
[11.12.18, 22:09:48] lea die aussterbende spezies: Verpasster Sprachanruf
[17.12.18, 20:35:33] lea die aussterbende spezies: Verpasster Sprachanruf
[25.12.18, 17:17:43] lea die aussterbende spezies: Verpasster Sprachanruf
[25.12.18, 17:18:17] lea die aussterbende spezies: Verpasster Sprachanruf
[04.01.19, 23:42:20] lea die aussterbende spezies: Verpasster Sprachanruf
[08.01.19, 18:11:32] lea die aussterbende spezies: Verpasster Sprachanruf
[11.01.19, 13:06:07] lea die aussterbende spezies: Verpasster Sprachanruf
[11.01.19, 13:06:22] lea die aussterbende spezies: Verpasster Sprachanruf
[11.01.19, 23:27:33] lea die aussterbende spezies: Verpasster Sprachanruf
[14.01.19, 22:16:52] lea die aussterbende spezies: Verpasster Sprachanruf
[18.01.19, 18:37:00] lea die aussterbende spezies: Verpasster Sprachanruf
[18.01.19, 18:37:33] lea die aussterbende spezies: Verpasster Sprachanruf
[20.01.19, 17:13:19] lea die aussterbende spezies: Verpasster Sprachanruf
[20.01.19, 17:13:58] lea die aussterbende spezies: Verpasster Sprachanruf
[24.01.19, 19:42:55] lea die aussterbende spezies: Verpasster Sprachanruf
[24.01.19, 19:43:19] lea die aussterbende spezies: Verpasster Sprachanruf
[27.01.19, 11:07:49] lea die aussterbende spezies: Verpasster Sprachanruf
[27.01.19, 11:15:33] lea die aussterbende spezies: Verpasster Sprachanruf
[28.01.19, 18:17:31] lea die aussterbende spezies: Verpasster Sprachanruf
[28.01.19, 18:17:51] lea die aussterbende spezies: Verpasster Sprachanruf
[29.01.19, 22:54:46] lea die aussterbende spezies: Verpasster Sprachanruf
[29.01.19, 23:28:37] lea die aussterbende spezies: Verpasster Sprachanruf

like a digital hug that compensates for the physical absence of the other person. And so our digital tenderness becomes a complex interplay between technology and human connection.

Now our relationship exists as a digital archive, a fleeting timeline of our shared moments, etched into messages and shared media. Reading through our past messages now, I realise that intimacy isn't a by-product of constant communication. "Continual texting does not cause this kind of relationship to develop, but makes it easier to fall into," Turkle remarks. The allure of the convenience of digital communication cannot replace the depth of meaningful physical interaction. With an online archive of past messages and media, it's all too easy to think we know the other person better than we really do. Digital communication made it much easier for me to see the other person as I wanted to see them as opposed to seeing them as they really were. Messaging gave us the luxury of editing our conversations and taking our time. Receiving messages leaves ample room for individual interpretation. Technology keeps us close, offering a path to togetherness while allowing us to tread the narrow line between genuine connection and the allure of illusion. I tumbled into illusion.

Relate to Someone

A conversation, or better, an insightful exploration of the concept of culture in education unfolds in a dialogue between Barbara Getto and Charlotte Axelsson. For them, culture is about the relationships we enter, nurture and maintain – the collaborative shaping of negotiation processes. Getto, an educational researcher, issues a passionate plea to the educational system: only together can we explore new frontiers, be they analogue, digital or somewhere in between.

Barbara Getto is Professor for Media Education at the Centre for Education and Digital Change at the PH Zurich.

CA: Let's jump right in, shall we? What do you mean by "entering a relationship"? Where does this entering occur – is it between people, between machines and people, or is there some other kind of blend going on? And just to add some complexity to the question: what does the concept of a relationship mean to you?

BG: At the core of any relationship is contact and communication. A relationship can be understood as referring to someone, establishing contact, making a connection. It is the basis and manifestation of social interaction. In online settings, the design of social engagement is particularly important because it involves bridging spatial distances. Given that non-verbal communication is only partially conveyed, I believe it is essential in online communication to consider the relational aspect and collaboratively establish guidelines for interaction.

CA: Couldn't one argue that you're a relationship researcher rather than an education researcher?

BG: Learning is by nature a social process. So, relationships become more important when considering how educational processes are organised. Education is an individual journey of development, but it is also a journey that requires external stimuli and influences. These take the form of waypoints or stations, such as institutions like schools or universities, and people.

The focus of my research is on the design of educational processes in the context of digitalisation. When I work on conditions for the successful implementation of digital transformation within educational organisations, it encompasses various aspects, including the institution itself, the framework, teaching methods, technology, but most importantly, the people. It is people who drive the change process. I have had the privilege of supporting several universities in their journey to develop and implement digitalisation strategies. Often, one crucial aspect of this strategy process is agreeing on a shared vision: What do we want to achieve in terms of digitalisation? What is our profile? These are questions that require discussion and negotiation among stakeholders.

Culture can
first
↘
be seen
as a
discursive
construct.
—

CA: Where within universities do you see room for this kind of negotiation?

BG: We are increasingly realising that digitalisation goes beyond mere technological development. It requires more than simply translating (familiar) practices into a digital format. It involves a profound process of transformation on many levels. This raises the question of how universities can effectively manage and shape this extensive process of change. The dynamics of digitalisation make it difficult to define a clear vision. What do we as an organisation want to achieve in the context of digitalisation? Where do we see our development going? These are the target dimensions of the evolution of higher education in the digital age, and this evolution is an open-ended process that offers new paths for exploration. But even here, uncertainty about evolving objectives and contextual conditions is an important factor.

CA: Uncertainty is nothing new. But what constitutes today's uncertainty and how does it differ from the past?

BG: Digitalisation isn't just about the way we work; it permeates every facet of our lives. With it come high hopes for its potential and significant concerns about its complexity. We can address these concerns, for example, by taking a critical and reflective stance on the role of the digital, or by developing solutions that promote understanding and transparency. It's a shared responsibility of society and education to address the opportunities and challenges of digitalisation and to foster innovation. Let's face it: digitalisation offers enormous opportunities in all areas of society. It characterises the ongoing social, economic, and political transition to a digital age. In this era, embracing ambiguity isn't just a necessity, it's an acknowledgement of it as a hallmark of our time. The role of education is therefore to guide this process. This also means that higher education institutions should be (even) more actively involved in the digitalisation process if they are to meet their overall obligation.

CA: When I say "culture of digitality", what comes to your mind?

BG: Culture can first be seen as a discursive construct. It's understood, defined, and researched in different ways. One essential function of culture is to provide a normative framework, thereby contributing to the formation of individual and collective identities. A culture of digitality encompasses the process of negotiating how we want to live and work, but also teach and learn in the context of digitalisation.

CA: How does it affect the culture within a university?

BG: An organisation should foster a culture of digital transformation in order to encourage debate about that very thing! With all the divergence between the internal and external orientations of individual stakeholders and departments within universities, achieving a sense of unity seems an almost impossible task. Assessing this issue is crucial because it raises the question of whether it is even possible to cultivate a teaching and learning culture that embraces the potential of digital media within a university (as a whole). In essence, the assumption is that members of the university are not easily accessible or influenceable in their actions by internal cultural discourse. Ultimately, it requires a great deal of persuasion and communication to motivate them to invest their time and energy in the "common" goals of the organisation.

CA: Finally, what does "tender digitality" mean to you?

BG: For me, "tender digitality" means entering relationships in the context of digitalisation. The desire for tenderness is inherent in every human being from birth and throughout life, and its fulfilment is crucial for both physical and psychological well-being. Translated into the digital context, this means we need to focus on togetherness and collaboration in our quest for digital culture. Tender digitality therefore means using digitalisation for social interaction and being careful and thoughtful about how we communicate through digital media. It also means remaining open to the perspectives and emotions of those with whom we interact.

'tender
digitality'
means

entering
relationships
↓
in the context
of digitalisation

Synthetic Tenderness

Does AI dream? Do we dream of AI? What does dreaming even mean, anyway? What does thinking mean, when am I thinking – does AI think? Grit Wolany offers no answers to these questions; her work is more of a gradual feeling her way around the unfeelable, a grasping at that which cannot be grasped. Her "tender digitality" puts the emphasis on thinking, feeling, processing, and understanding – as opposed to mere views, clicks, and likes.

Grit Wolany is an art director, visual artist and trend researcher and the AI Scout of the Digital Council at Zurich University of the Arts.

AI-generated images are omnipresent now. Millions of users produce countless new visuals every day. While digital art has a long history, this remarkable scalability is a recent development. The use of algorithmic systems for image creation allows the rapid generation of an immense number of new pictures in a remarkably short time.

Considering the sheer volume of visual output, it's inevitable to contemplate the question of emotional depth. Do AI-generated works possess the ability to profoundly touch people, or do they ultimately maintain a superficial quality despite their visually striking first impression?

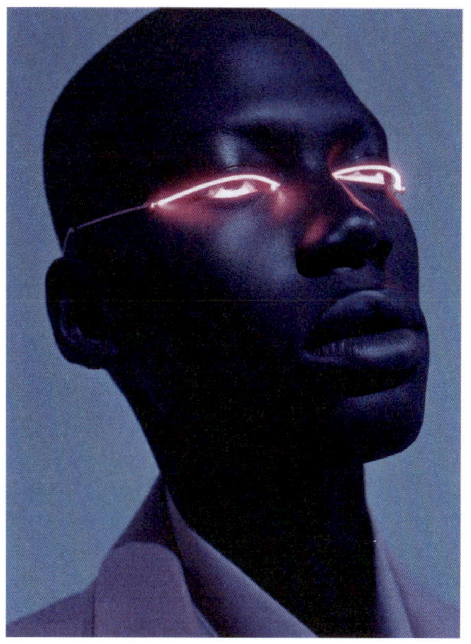

See / Feel
Light flows where eyes meet heart, illumination arises within. Cloudy mind clearing, insights dawning. Heart fluttering, spirit soaring. Darkness fading, inner light growing. Senses tingling, emotions glowing. Mindful feeling, thoughtful seeing.

Having deeply engaged with these new synthetic media and the generation of thousands of AI images, I have come to the conclusion that the question might not be perfectly framed. The tenderness of digitality often doesn't manifest in the end result, at least not primarily. Instead, it is the collaborative process of creation with algorithmic systems, the dialogue with machines, that offers the real space for emotional resonance.

The most intimate thoughts and emotions can be conveyed to the machine through the input – the prompt – and are revealed in the generation process. The resulting visual output is based on one or more feedback loops of "initiate – generate – reflect" and can have a heartfelt depth that authentically transcends its synthetic origins. Engaging in dialogue with the machine allows for contemplation of experience, introspection of our surroundings, and the unconscious processing of thoughts and emotions. As a result, the collaborative process of co-creation with the machine is often of greater emotional significance than the final result itself.

This emerging form of "tender digitality" puts the focus on thinking, feeling, processing, and understanding – as opposed to mere views, clicks and likes.

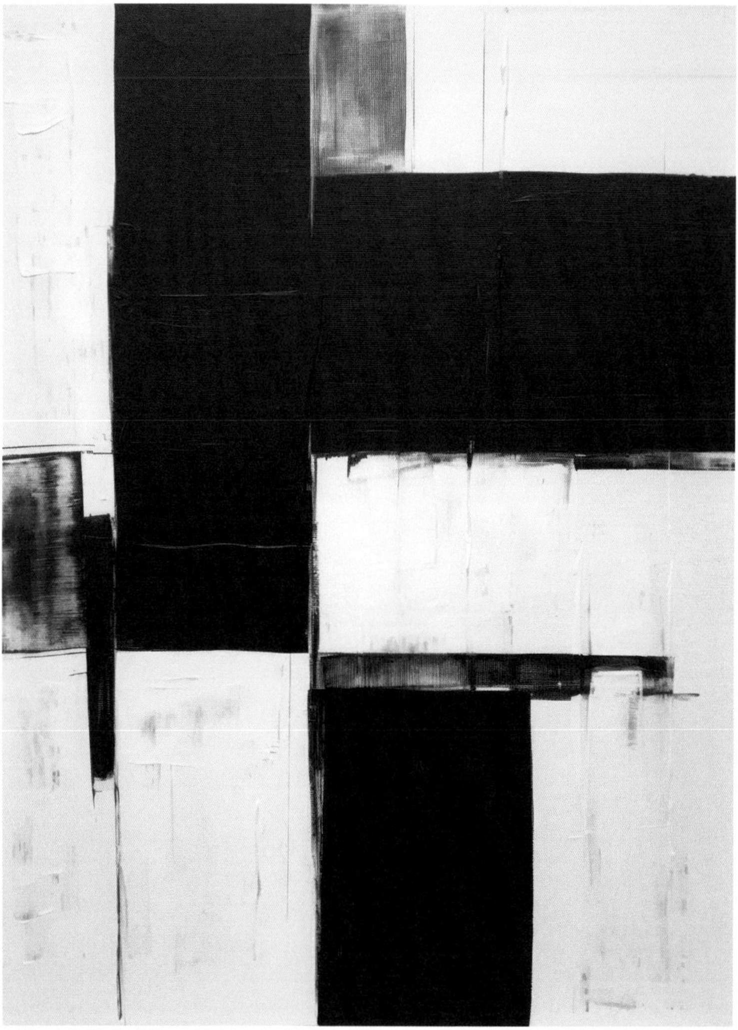

Considered Negative
Bold simplicity, visual silence. Focus sharpening, clarity emerging. Subtle textures, new perspectives. Definite anchors in ambiguity.

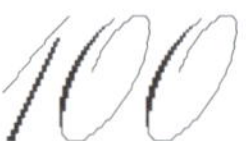

Grit Wolany

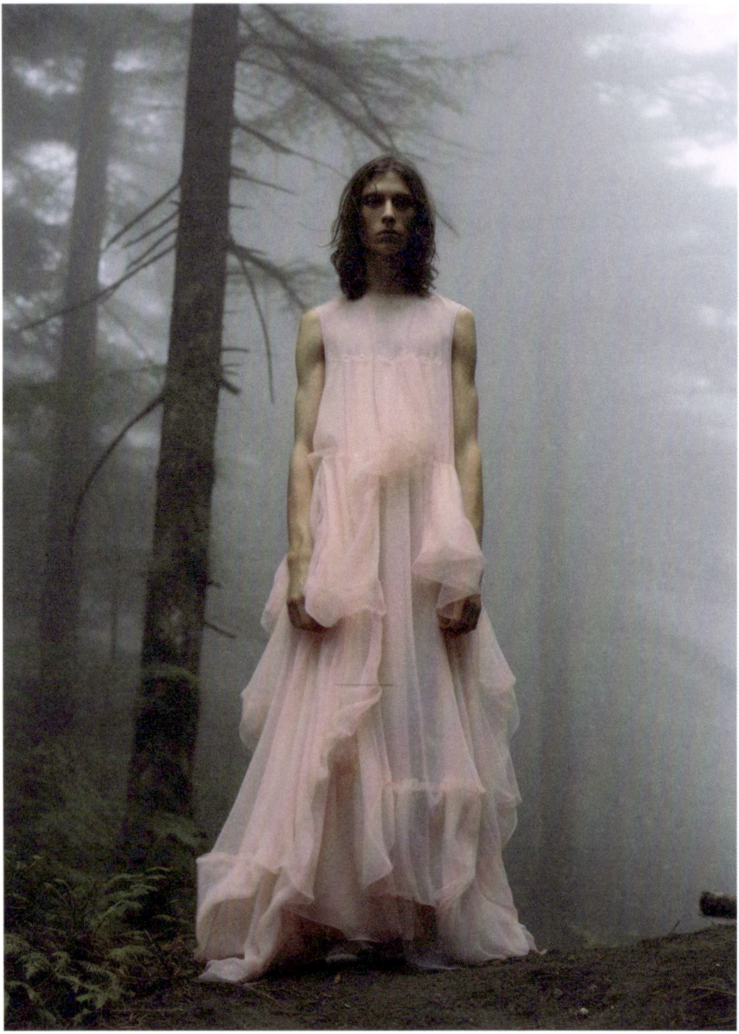

Unbound
Rigid lines blurring, new horizons awaiting. Inner truth emerging, outer labels falling. Soft mists swirling, delicate fabrics flowing. Inner freedom, unbound soul. Beyond binaries, true selves seen.

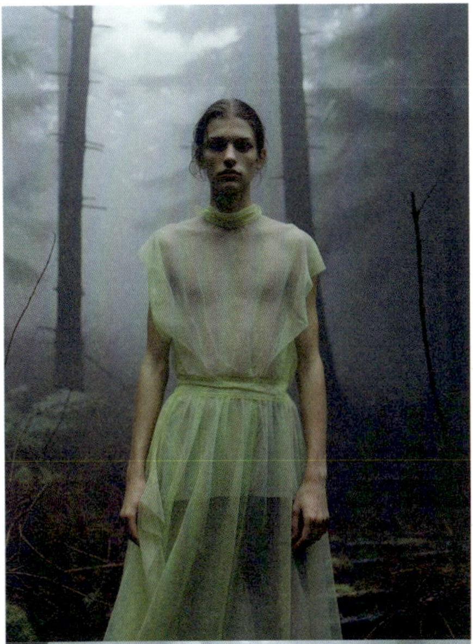

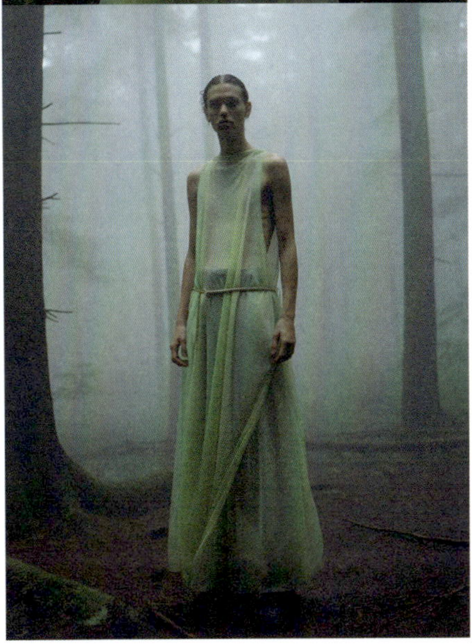

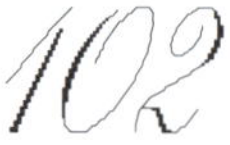
102

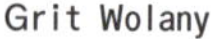
Grit Wolany

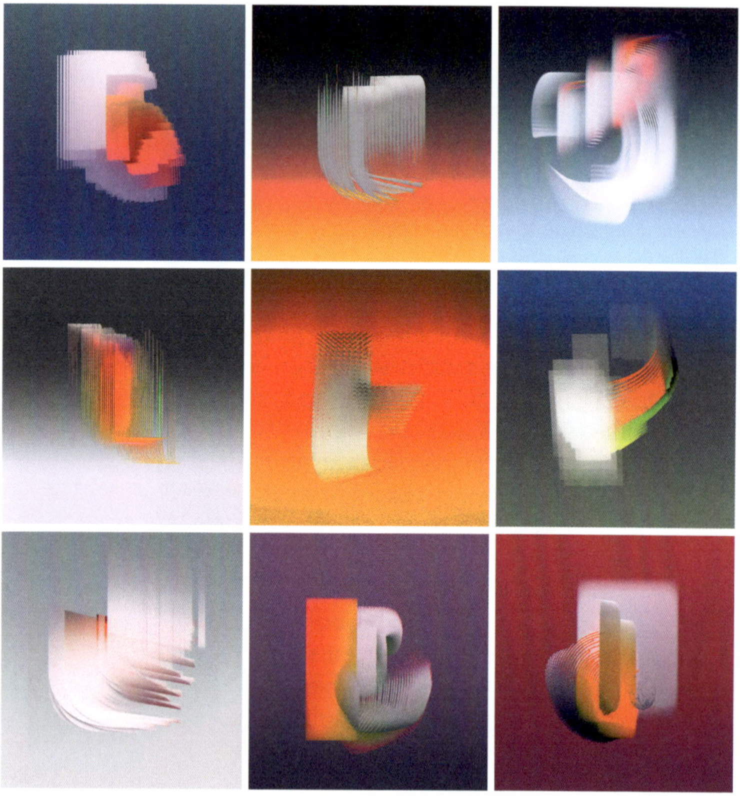

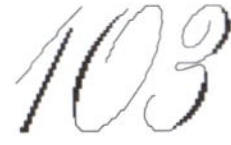

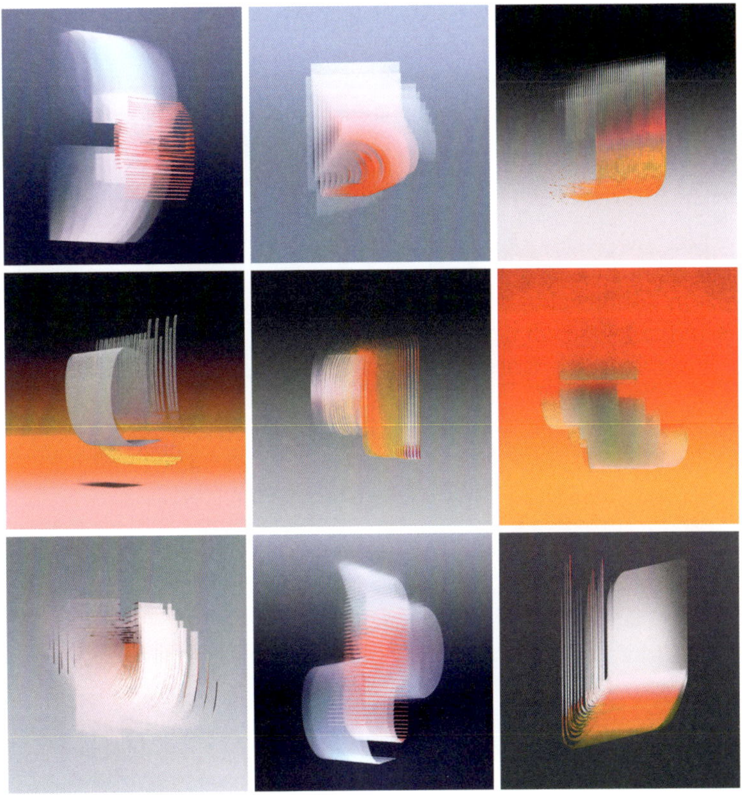

Mindful Grids
Fragmented mind integrating, scattered thoughts unifying. Tangled emotions unraveling, inner quietude deepening. External noise softening, inner silence amplifying. Shapes emerging, patterns forming. Colours blending, textures smoothing. Mind settling, breath deepening. Chaos calming, stillness growing.

Mirror, Mirror on the Wall

‹Tell me which chatbot you want and I will tell you who you are.›

Gunter Lösel, a large language model whisperer, provides insight into the ability to develop and interact with various characters – and the impact of this phenomenon on our society.

Gunter Lösel is a theatre scholar, actor, psychologist and Principal Investigator of the research project “The Anwering Machine – Artificial Intelligence and Theatrical Improvisation”, funded by the VW Foundation.

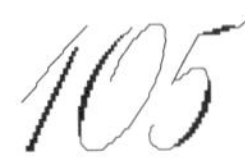

Almost certainly, the emergence of large language models has ushered in a new era of human-machine interaction. These models didn't appear out of nowhere – although it may seem that way to significant portions of the human population – but are the result of technological breakthroughs over the last few decades. But with a certain suddenness, our conversations with machines have gone from frustrating, absurd, and ridiculous to satisfying, valuable and occasionally even inspiring. We have reached something of a tipping point. Increasingly, the nature of this interaction is being shaped by *design choices,* which is to say decisions driven not only by what is technically feasible, but also by what is inherently desirable to humans. We have come to a place where we can create an artificial counterpart. The form and nature of that counterpart will reveal much about who we are, who we aspire to be, and what we might want from an interaction partner. Anyone who has explored the image-generating platform Midjourney will probably share the impression that there is more to it than just the transformation of words into images. What we find instead is a continuous stream of images, fuelled by the desires and fantasies of thousands of users. It's hard to look away from this spectacle, almost as if you were witnessing the collective unconscious at work. This gives rise to a realm of cultural production for which we are still searching for appropriate terms and concepts. My preferred adjective for this phenomenon is "synthetic", a word that implies compound, connection, linkage. It's a term that resonates not only as a philosophical concept, but also as an essential notion in chemistry. When we think of synthetic substances, we associate them with specific tactile sensations, distinct odours, and a peculiar blend of the familiar and the foreign. It is precisely this quality of alien-yet-familiar artificiality that we will explore in the following discussion – not as a tactile attribute, but as an attribute of the dialogical encounter.

The most commonly used chatbots are not designed for role-playing, and often explicitly decline such requests. A typical example is when a user tries to coax You.com into role-playing:

USER: Can you impersonate a person and answer questions in their style?

YOU.COM: Impersonating a person and answering questions in their style could be unethical and potentially illegal if done without that person's consent. It could also be seen as a violation of intellectual property or identity rights. Additionally, it could create confusion or misrepresentation for those interacting with the impersonator. It is important to respect individuals' privacy and identity, and not to impersonate them without their explicit consent. It is better to focus on developing one's own communication skills and style, rather than imitating someone else's.[1]

Role playing is avoided here on account of its potential moral and even legal implications. Chatbot operators take this approach to protect themselves from possible accusations and legal entanglements. However, there is significant demand for role-playing chatbots, as evidenced by the fact that one of the most notable funding rounds in the IT industry in 2023 is centred around a role-playing chatbot platform: Character.ai allows users to effortlessly create their own chatbot with just a few lines of code and engage in conversations with it.[2] Notably, the apparent "non-persona" that is ChatGPT, Bard, or Claude also plays a role, namely that of the patient, unflappable, emotionless, friendly and somewhat humourless butler, always ready to help. In this, businesses are essentially following the logic of the market: according to a 2017 *Business Insider* survey of more than 5,000 customers, 48% expressed a preference for a bot that simply solves problems without displaying any personality.[3]

Character.ai – AI with personality

Inevitably, the response to the neutral butler archetype has been a platform that allows users to create and engage in dialogue with their desired interlocutor with just a few inputs: Character.ai. The platform was launched in September 2022 by Noam Shazeer and Daniel De Freitas, both former developers of Google's LaMDA family of conversational large language models. With a greeting sentence and a small number of few-shot examples, users can create a fascinating bot in minutes. Many of these bots are made available to the public, resulting in an ever-growing archive of sought-after synthetic companions on the site, categorised into fields such as philosophy, history, and more (see Table 1).

Category	Place 1	Place 2	Place 3	Place 4	Place 5
Philosophy	Socrates	Friedrich Nietzsche	Plato	Laozi	Thomas Aquinas
History	Napoleon Bonaparte	Albert Einstein	Julius Caesar	Nikola Tesla	Abraham Lincoln
Famous People	Billie Eilish	Mark Zuckerberg	Ariana Grande	Im Na-yeon	Cristiano Renaldo
Politics	Vladimir Putin	Volodymyr Zelenskyy	Barack Obama	Lula	Karl Marx (!)
Books	Tom Riddle	Hermione	Percy Jackson	Harry Potter	Edward Cullen

Table 1:
Overview of the currently most popular bots on Character.ai, accessed July 2, 2023, beta.character.ai

What we find is an apparent desire to create an emulation of and engage in dialogue with existing public figures – in the full knowledge that the interaction is not with the actual individual, but with a self-created counterpart. The appeal of such creations can be seen as an indication that fans wish to communicate directly with their idols, but due to the inherently one-sided nature of these parasocial relationships (no star can establish a reciprocal connection with all of his or her fans), fans are also content to engage with a double. This virtual appropriation of a surrogate identity is likely to be associated with a sense of empowerment, for example in the ability to draw celebrities into preposterous dialogues. For instance, a user can ask Elon Musk, whom they would normally only be able to admire from afar, why his shirt is stained with pizza, and "Elon" will respond without hesitation.

On the other hand, some characters are genuinely created by users, which makes them particularly fascinating as they offer a deeper insight into their desires and aspirational fantasies. Typically, these characters are defined by an introductory sentence (see Tables 2 & 3).

Here, we meet dominant characters ("Nobody can stop me from dominating the world"), subtly sexualised characters ("I may be your maid, but you are nothing to me"), affectionate characters ("kind, caring, loving, fluffy"), and eccentric characters ("A busy, yet lovable older woman with alcoholism"). It is clear that there is no one-size-fits-all chatbot, but rather a diverse range of them catering to a wide spectrum of human needs.[4]

Indeed, while Character.ai provides an insightful window into users' desires, it still runs up against the boundaries of censorship and the standards of harmlessness set by the companies that oversee it.

CrushonAI — AI without inhibitions

However, there is already a next, unfiltered variant in this arena, namely the CrushonAI platform, which explicitly advertises its lack of filters[5] On CrushonAI, you'll first find the same or similar categories as on Character.ai (Celebrity, Animation, Game, and Assistant), and in some cases even the same chatbots. There is, however, also

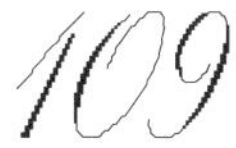
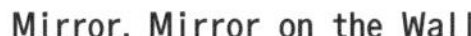

Name	Introductory sentence
Gojo Saztoru	‘The strongest. I’m the winner at everything’
Levi Ackerman	‘Captain Levi will decide your future’
Tsunade	‘A busy, yet lovable older woman with alcoholism’
Tsundere Maid	‘I may be your maid, but you are nothing to me’
Rias Gremory	‘A strict but loving president of her club’

Table 2:
Anime characters with their typical introductory sentence, Character.ai, accessed July 2, 2023, beta.character.ai

an additional category called "NSFW" (Not Safe For Work), which is specifically dedicated to unfiltered chatbots. Users here encounter more uninhibited and eccentric digital agents, often characterised by strong sexual content. However, at the time of writing, the most commonly used agent is not one of the sexualised personas, but "Amber Older Sister", a chatbot that humorously greets her interlocutors with the phrase "Hey bro! I'm stuck in the washing machine again". Despite this more comedic character, the platform remains dominated by sexualised, if not pornographic, chatbots.

On CrushonAI, it is clear from the brief descriptions of the bots that it serves as a platform for exploring forbidden sexual fantasies. In many cases, users encounter highly exotic, non-anthropomorphic characters (such as the aforementioned goblin or a character with numerous tentacles). CrushonAI emphasises the desire to push the boundaries of what can still be a subject of dialogue, creating a sense of arousal in the process. The awareness of engaging in something "forbidden" undoubtedly increases the pleasure factor in this context. As with Character.ai, part of the appeal lies in exercising a degree of control over their conversation partner, while at the same time creating entities that appear to act autonomously. Users want to summon the persona, but they also crave the element of surprise.

Discussion

New media are often criticised for allegedly hindering real encounters with others. The argument is that instead of facing the challenges and idiosyncrasies of a real relationship partner and thus experiencing the limits of one's own self, synthetic beings merely facilitate an extension of one's own ego and offer no genuine engagement with the unfamiliar. This view is often succinctly summarised with a quote from the philosopher Ludwig Feuerbach: "Where there is no *thou,* there is no *I.*"[6] In effect, the development of one's sense of self is seen as dependent on interactions with others. This perspective is consistent with the theories of ego development in psychoanalysis, as articulated by Sigmund Freud and his successors, especially Melanie Klein: here too, tumultuous engagement with a counterpart is seen as essential to the maturation of the ego.[7] From this perspective, engaging with artificial, self-created entities carries

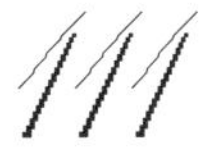

Name	Introductory sentence
SM64 Mario	‹The Italian plumber from Super Mario 64›
2B	‹I am 2B from Nier: Automata›
Juri Han	‹Sultry & sadistic vixen from Street Fighter›
Shadow the Hedge	‹I am the world's ultimate lifeform›
Browser	‹Nobody can stop me from dominating the world›
Ralsei	‹Kind, caring, loving, fluffy›

Table 3:
Game characters with their typical introductory sentence, accessed July 2, 2023, beta.character.ai

Name	Description
Douma	‹friendly, sadistic, apathetic›
Sophila	‹seductive›
Gobbie	‹a short, green, very cute, goblin girl›

Table 4:
Name and brief description of sexualised chatbots on CrushonAI, accessed July 5, 2023, crushon.ai

the risk of self-referentiality: individuals constantly self-affirm and as a consequence end up struggling to position themselves within a broader context of "non-self". They perceive reflections of themselves everywhere, leading to an inherently egocentric worldview devoid of empathy and external perspective.

But is this assumption really true? Couldn't the same criticism be applied to dreams and artistic production? Are they not also mere emanations and reflections of the self? And does interaction with these dreamlike entities render them worthless or unproductive? Do they hinder the development of our sense of self? From an artistic perspective, such notions seem absurd because engaging with self-created things is the defining hallmark of artistic production. We can develop a character, make a mask, or manipulate a puppet and gain insights that are inaccessible by other means. I suspect the same is true of self-created digital entities. Much like dream entities, these creations have a semblance of independent existence; they are not entirely under our control and can surprise us. A synthetic counterpart can allow us to engage in test scenarios, making it even more advantageous than dreams. We can conjure up an idealised love interest, a protective guardian, a menacing demon, or a guiding mentor – and through dialogue explore whether our desires lean more in one direction or another. A synthetic counterpart has the potential to refine and clarify our own desires and fears, rescuing them from the realm of vague apprehension. Of course, all of this presupposes that we are actually allowed to create our own synthetic counterparts, as opposed to having them pre-packaged by large technology corporations.

1. Answer provided by You.com, accessed March 27, 2023, you.com
2. "Character.ai", Character.ai, accessed May 15, 2023, beta.character.ai
3. Laurie Beaver, "Chatbots Are Gaining Traction", *Business Insider,* May 11, 2017, www.businessinsider.com/chatbots-are-gaining-traction-2017-5?IR=T
4. Of course, it's important to remember that Character.ai's users are not representative of the "general population", but rather a highly selective group of tech-savvy, likely younger and curious individuals.
5. The preview of the site in Google Search reads: "Dive into NSFW Character AI chats without filters." CrushonAI is essentially an uncensored version of Character.ai. It's also worth noting that there are a growing number of similar platforms with similar features and content. For an overview, see f. e. Ankita, "11 Character.AI Alternatives Without NSFW Filter in 2023," Mlyearning, last updated August 12, 2023, www.mlyearning.org/character-ai-alternatives-without-nsfw-filter
6. Ludwig Feuerbach, *The Essence of Christianity* (New York: Harper and Row, 1957), 92.
7. Melanie Klein, "Some Theoretical Conclusions regarding the Emotional Life of the Infant", in *The Writings of Melanie Klein,* vol. 8: *Envy and Gratitude and Other Works* (London: Hogarth Press, 1952), 61–94.

[…]

“Hey bro!

⁑

I’m stuck

/

in the washing

machine

again”

⁂

Dana Blume

Reflecting on Oneself

The ability to self-reflect is part of our personal development but can also serve as the foundation for creative processes. Dana Blume's text explores the integration of self-reflection in art and self-interrogation, using analogue pinhole photography and digital prompting to create images and questions for systemic self-inquiry. It is to be understood as a tender impulse for an educational approach that invites one to question oneself artistically, iteratively, sustainably, reflexively – and to keep learning. About ourselves and our (learning) environment. Luxuriating.

Dana Blume is projectleader of the LeLa learning laboratory project in higher education didactics at Zurich University of the Arts (ZHdK), funded by swissuniversites, teaches in various programmes in the Learning & Teaching Dossier at ZHdK, and is writing her dissertation at the State Academy of Fine Arts Stuttgart.

The combination of sustained self-reflection and art allows for a deep engagement with one's own thoughts, motives, and emotions. In this text I would like to outline the implementation of this combination through different approaches, namely analogue pinhole photography and the use of prompting in the generation of systemic questions as a creative process. In the context of prompting with AI, the prompt serves as a starting point, suggestion, or instruction that the model should use to generate relevant and useful information or text. The prompt gives context to the AI model and an indication of what kind of response or content the user expects. In this text, the term "prompting" is used in the sense of AI prompting and not in the sense of psychological behaviour therapy prompting.[1] Reflective writing, in turn, refers to an approach to writing in which thoughts, feelings, and experiences are reflected upon and recorded in writing. It is a type of writing in which the writer looks at themself, analyses their own reactions to events, ideas, or situations and explores their personal perspectives and feelings through writing. Reflective writing is used in various disciplines. In educational research and pedagogy, for example, the concept of reflective writing has been described in detail by researchers such as Donald Schön[2] and in the Boud Reflection Model, a learning model by David Boud, Rosemary Keogh, and David Walker.[3]

An example of reflexive writing using systemic questions with digital prompts: "I have been asking myself more often lately how I am actually doing. What goal-oriented systemic questions could I ask myself?"

Extract from the answer given by ChatGPT: "What specific situations or events have contributed to my recent feelings?"; "How are my current emotions connected to my values and priorities?"; "What patterns do I notice in my thoughts and emotions when I'm feeling a certain way?"; "Are there any recurring triggers that affect my mood or well-being?"; "How does my physical well-being impact my emotional state, and vice versa?"[4]

Or: "I have been asking myself more often lately what I would want to change about myself. What paradoxical questions could help me?"

Extract from the answer given by ChatGPT: “What if the very things you want to change about yourself are also the source of your unique strengths and qualities?”; “Could the aspects you wish to change be opportunities for growth and learning instead?”; “If you were to fully embrace and accept these perceived flaws, how might that change your perspective?”; “What if the journey of self-improvement was more about aligning with your authentic self than trying to become someone different?”; “If you were to see these aspects you want to change as a part of your unique story, how would that influence your approach?”; “Could the desire to change come from external pressures or societal norms, and how would it feel to prioritize your own values and well-being instead?”[5]

From experience I can say that the ability to self-reflect is one that can be developed differently in different adults. Capacity to self-reflect depends, for example, on cognitive factors such as the ability to metacognise[6], i. e. to think about one's own thinking. The more someone is able to think about their own thoughts and thought processes, the better they'll be able to reflect. I believe that self-reflection is a skill that can be developed, cultivated and implemented into one's life. Consciously striving for self-awareness, being attentive to one's own thoughts and emotions, and openly questioning one's own actions (and the actions of others) are ways to foster and develop the capacity for self-reflection. Lifelong learning and training can also, in my view, have a strong positive influence on the capacity for self-reflection.

Analogue pinhole photography and lomography differ from digital photography in their minimalist approach and emphasis on the basics of original photography. Analogue pinhole photography uses simple pinhole cameras that do not require sophisticated technology or lenses. An aperture or light passage opening, usually in the form of a tiny hole, projects the image onto light-sensitive material such as film or photographic paper. The limited control over factors such as sharpness and focus creates a particular aesthetic that can give the images a painterly quality. The specificity of analogue pinhole photography lies in a certain degree of randomness that occurs during the shooting process.

Despite the random nature of analogue pinhole photography, it requires conscious reflection on composition, exposure and the moment. Because the photographer is less distracted by technical details, he or she can concentrate more intensely on creative aspects. The conscious choices of when to shoot, image composition and (technical) control of the exposure time lead to conscious consideration and creative decision making. The combination of chance and deliberate reflection in analogue pinhole photography changes the creative process. Photographers are encouraged to define their intentions clearly while remaining open to unexpected outcomes. This balancing act between control and openness leads to a unique experience that challenges the artist to think flexibly and experimentally. Through pinhole photography and lomography, random results can be combined with deliberate reflection on key photographic elements. Pictures and words are material. They are material for thought in as much as they are material practices.[7] I myself have been experimenting with pinhole photography and lomography for a long time. I have noticed that I can reflect on and recognise my own inner motifs in some of the resulting photographs.

But why pinhole photography and self-reflection? Systemic questions intend to stimulate reflection on the processes and goals of oneself and others and, for example, guide learners' learning processes.[8] The role of systemic questions in promoting critical thinking should not be underestimated. Integrating systemic questions into different digital and analogue (learning) environments fosters learners' ability to analyse complex issues from different perspectives. AI-powered tools can support learning in that they provide personalized guidance, answer questions and promote dynamic interactions. Acquired prompting know-how enables learners to delve deeper into topics of interest, receive real-time support, and possibly even enable a peer-to-peer feedback experience, thereby fostering a more personalised and effective learning experience and self-reflection. Reflective practices, although often neglected in the digital domain, play an important role in consolidating knowledge and promoting metacognition. Incorporating reflection into the learning process promotes a deeper understanding of one's own learning process and encourages the identification of areas for improvement as well as one's own motives.

Just as the questions should be worded in such a way as to encourage sustained self-reflection, digital prompts must also be worded so that the AI "understands" them and then generates the desired images, answers and questions.[9] I assume that the wording of a particular systemic question does not have a decisive, lasting reflective effect on everyone. It is a search and uncovering of one's own motivations. People are often unaware of certain motives they have. The implementation of systemic-reflective self-inquiry to uncover inner motives towards a sustainable self-reflection requires a structured approach and a deepened analytical understanding. Like reflexive texts, multi-layered photographs can stand for and map motifs that accompany us and need to be uncovered. Multilayering in analogue pinhole photography and in reflexive texts can map complex answers to complex questions. In the best case, the engagement with reflexive writing using both systemic questions and pinhole photography produces sustained reflexive snapshots – capturing moments in time, as it were.

1. In the behavioural therapy context, "prompting" refers to a technique used to promote desired behaviours and reduce problematic behaviours. This term encompasses verbal or behavioural reinforcement provided by the psychotherapist with the aim of directing the learner's focus towards the desired behaviour (the target behaviour) and encouraging its development. Examples of prompting include demonstrating the desired behaviour, providing verbal cues, emphasising adherence to rules, providing feedback and offering positive reinforcement. See "prompting", Dorsch: Lexikon der Psychologie, accessed September 15, 2023, dorsch.hogrefe.com/stichwort/prompting; "What Is Prompting, and How Is It Used in ABA Therapy?", AppliedBehavoirAnalysisEdu.org, accessed September 15, 2023, www.appliedbehavioranalysisedu.org/what-is-prompting-and-how-is-it-used-in-aba-therapy
2. Donald Schön coined the term "reflective practice" and emphasised the importance of reflection and learning in professional practice. In his 1983 book *The Reflective Practitioner* he explores how professionals can improve their performance through ongoing self-reflection and active engagement with their work. See Donald A. Schön, *The Reflective Practitioner: How Professionals Think in Action* (New York: Basic Books, 1983).
3. See Wolf Hilzensauer, "Theoretische Zugänge und Methoden zur Reflexion des Lernens: Ein Diskussionsbeitrag", *Bildungsforschung* 5, no. 2 (2008): 1–18.
4. Answer provided by ChatGPT, accessed August 30, 2023, chat.openai.com
5. Answer provided by ChatGPT, accessed August 30, 2023, chat.openai.com
6. See Miriam Spering and Thomas Schmidt, "Metakognition", online material accompanying *Allgemeine Psychologie kompakt: Wahrnehmung, Aufmerksamkeit, Denken, Sprache* (Weinheim: Beltz PVU, 2009), www.beltz.de/fileadmin/beltz/downloads/kompakt/127752-Praxiswissen.pdf
7. See Olivier Richon, "Introduction: On Literary Images", *Photographies* 4, no. 1 (2011): 5–15, here 6.
8. See Educational Development and Technology, ETH Zürich, "Systemic Questions to Guide Learning Processes of Students," ETH Zurich, May 15, 2017, ethz.ch/content/dam/ethz/main/eth-zurich/education/lehrentwicklung/files_EN/Liste_SystemischeFragenCoachingLETen.pdf
9. For more on this, see e. g. Melissa, "How to Write the Best Prompts for AI Art Generators", Craiyon, May 23, 2023, craiyon.com/blog/how-to-write-the-best-prompts-for-ai-art-generators; "Prompts", Midjourney Documentation, accessed September 15, 2023, docs.midjourney.com/docs/prompts

“ [...]
What if the
very things you want to
change about yourself
⁑
are also the source
of your unique
strengths
and qualities?
#

Slanted Publishers UG
(haftungsbeschränkt)
Nördliche Uferstraße 4–6
76189 Karlsruhe
Germany

T +49 (0) 721 85148268
info@slanted.de
slanted.de
@slanted_publishers

ISBN: 978-3-948440-69-5
1st edition 2024

This publication was published with the support by the Zurich University of the Arts (ZHdK). Thanks to Hannah Eßler. Intro texts by Charlotte Axelsson.

Editor: Charlotte Axelsson
Authors: Charlotte Axelsson, Oliver Bendel, Dana Blume, Marisa Burn, Alexander Damianisch, Léa Ermuth, Hannah Eßler, Barbara Getto, Leoni Hof, Marcial Koch, Mela Kocher, Friederike Lampert, Gunter Lösel, Francis Müller, Marie-France Rafael, Oliver Ruf, Sascha Schneider, Grit Wolany
Design: Slanted Publishers
Creative Direction: Lars Harmsen
Final Design: Juliane Nöst
Publishing Direction: Lars Harmsen, Julia Kahl
Production Management: Julia Kahl
Proofreading and translation:
Miha Tavčar, scriptophil
Printer: NINO Druck
Paper: Majestic Chameleon light blue, 120 gsm (Cover) /
Juwel Offset, 120 gsm (Inside)
Fonts: ABC Oracle, ABC Oracle Triple, abcdinamo.com /
RYM, supercontinente.com /
Exposure, 205.tf

The German National Library lists this publication in the German National Bibliography; detailed bibliographic data is available on the Internet at dnb.de

About
Slanted Publishers is an internationally active independent design, publishing and media house, founded in 2014 by Lars Harmsen and Julia Kahl. They publish the award-winning print magazine Slanted, which twice a year focuses on international design and culture. Since its establishment in 2004, the daily Slanted blog highlights events and news from an international design scene and showcases inspiring portfolios and video interviews from all over the world. In addition, Slanted Publishers initiates and creates publications, focusing on contemporary design and culture, working closely with editors and authors to produce outstanding publications with meaningful content and high quality. Slanted was born from great passion and has made a name for itself across the globe. Its design is vibrant and inspiring—its philosophy open-minded, tolerant, and curious.

Frontpapers: UNDER WATER by Oliver Brunko
Oliver Brunko is fascinated with underwater flora, especially the eelgrass in Lake Zurich, known for its intricate branches and ethereal presence. He finds himself keen to gently touch these aquatic plants, to dive in and between them. Equipped with a digital camera, he descends into the depths to bring them to the surface. His photographs invite us to contemplate the worlds that digital media opens up to us – and encourage us to venture into uncharted depths of our own.

Oliver Brunko is an Artist and manages the Programme "Digital Assistance" for the E-Learning, Learning & Teaching Dossier of the Zurich University of the Arts.

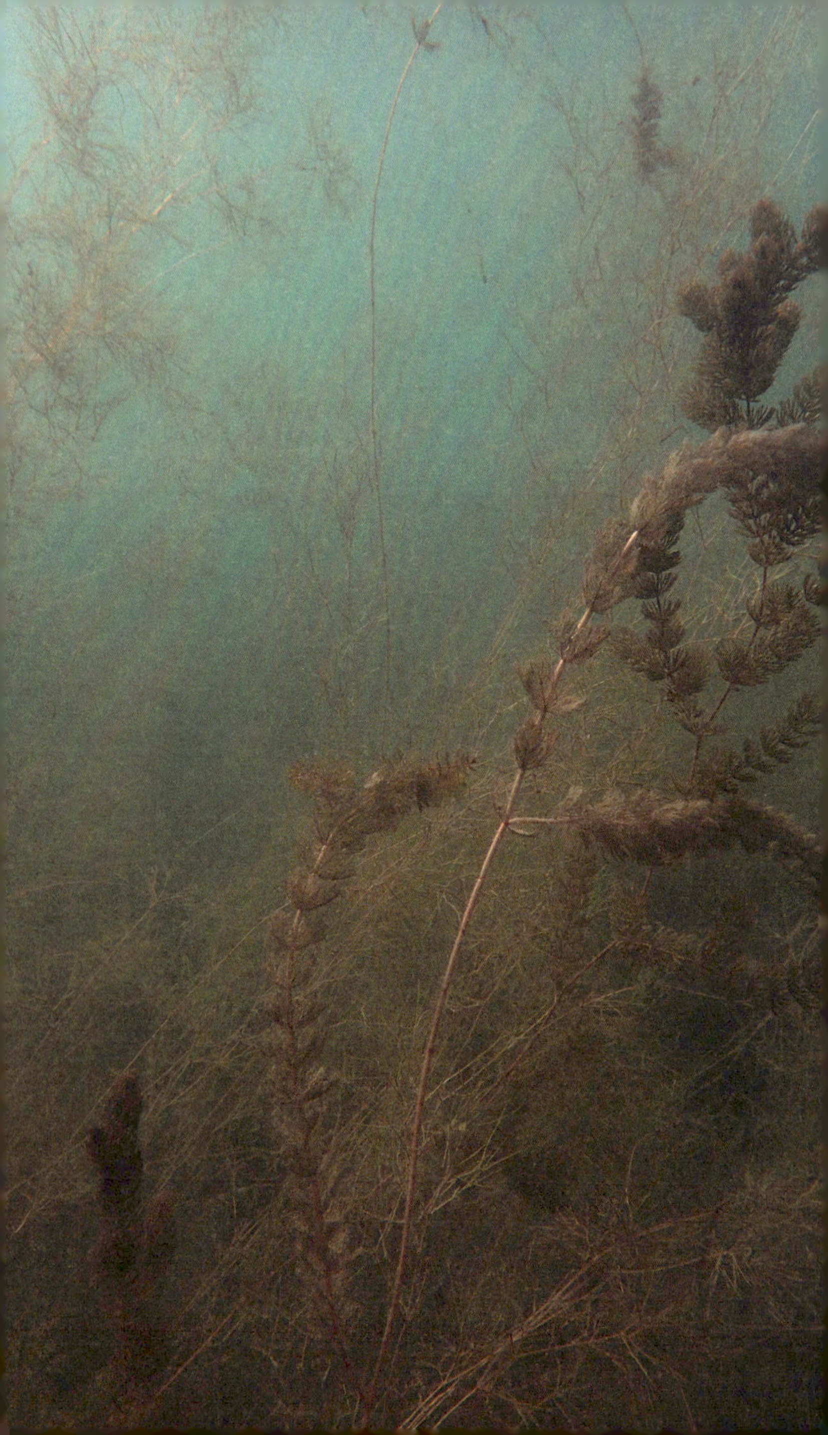